# ISAY WEINFELD
# WORKS

# ISAY WEINFELD
# WORKS

**Foreword by**
Agnaldo Farias

**Introduction by**
Isay Weinfeld

**Text by**
James Moore McCown

**Principal photography by**
Fernando Guerra

**Edited by**
Oscar Riera Ojeda

*RIZZOLI*
NEW YORK

New York · Paris · London · Milan

# CONTENTS

# FOREWORD

By Agnaldo Farias

**Agnaldo Farias** is a PhD professor at the School of Architecture and Urbanism at the University of São Paulo. He was Chief Curator of the Oscar Niemeyer Museum, the Tomie Ohtake Institute, and the Rio de Janeiro Museum of Modern Art. He was also Curator of Temporary Exhibitions at the Museum of Contemporary Art at the University of São Paulo. In terms of the São Paulo Biennial, he was Chief Curator of the 29th São Paulo Biennial, Chief Curator of the Brazilian Representation at the 25th São Paulo Biennial, and Deputy Curator of the 23rd São Paulo Biennial. He was Chief Curator of the 3rd Biennial of Coimbra, Portugal (2019), International Curator of the 11th Cuenca Biennial, Ecuador (2011), and Curator of the Brazilian Pavilion at the 54th edition of the Venice Biennale (2011).

For those who are accustomed to associating Brazilian architecture to its recent modern past—on the one hand, Oscar Niemeyer's plastic virtuosity, and on the other, the brutalist buildings with extensive use of exposed concrete, as seen in the designs of Vilanova Artigas and Paulo Mendes da Rocha—it is important to keep in mind that the work of Isay Weinfeld, who studied and graduated during a period when those lines of work were criticized, relates to other architectural trends and, above all, to other disciplines, including music, visual arts, and cinema. This is without overlooking Weinfeld's interest in other subjects, which is responsible for the practice of arranging courses and lectures at his office for himself and his employees about various subjects, ranging from psychoanalysis and Greek classics to recent developments in science.

Isay Weinfeld became an architect without knowing how to draw, a skill that architecture schools still consider indispensable. Weinfeld—an erratic student at Universidade Presbiteriana Mackenzie's (Mackenzie Presbyterian University) Architecture and Urbanism School, equally interested in the curricular requirements and the intense cultural offerings in the city of São Paulo in the 1970s—advocates that there are several ways of thinking and practicing architecture. In his case, he adopts a working process similar to that of an orchestra conductor (his teenage dream) or a film director. In any case, for him, an architect is someone with the imagination and ability to gather talented people to work under their coordination.

The reference to cinema is not incidental. Weinfeld, in association with colleague Marcio Kogan, directed one feature film that clearly demonstrates his deep identification with Jacques Tati. Add to that reference the familiarity with the filmography of Buñuel, Bergman, Fellini, and Kubrick, crucial for understanding his architecture as well as the objects it houses, which trigger the bodily choreographies of those who use them—transient users and dwellers.

From Weinfeld's point of view, the environments in a house, whatever they are, must stir emotions. A dining room, for instance, somehow resonates with the dining room that Luis Buñuel turned into a bathroom in *The Phantom of Liberty*; a staircase—any staircase—will connect to the one Gloria Swanson descends in Billy Wilder's *Sunset Boulevard*. No more, no less.

To better understand what s at play in Isay Weinfeld's work, one should examine not only his buildings, the streamlined plasticity in the volumes, the formal refinement, and the precision Weinfeld favors, but also the singularity of the treatment given to the environments, the textures on the walls, the calibrated lighting, the way a corridor draws attention to itself and pulls users into it, the choice and arrangement of furniture and other objects. Regarding the latter, it will be helpful to know about Weinfeld's artistic production, still little known although always practiced, the creation of ready-mades and assemblages resulting from the objects he has collected over decades wandering around flea markets, warehouses, and storerooms outside of time and space—objects that have stories, as well as those resulting from ultra-advanced technology, such as the Chinese sneaker he displayed under a glass dome at one of his latest exhibitions.

Weinfeld's attention to comfort is combined with imagination and a complex understanding of "dwelling" as a verb permeated by drama, whether a domestic, trivial drama, or the interpersonal relationships in an office—all imbued with affection and good humor. Ah, the good humor. This may be the most distinctive element of his long career. In his case, good humor rhymes with irony, with the ability to draw unexpected connections, mix syntagms, and articulate disparate signs and systems. It is a procedure that the better part of contemporary architecture, due to its preference for looking only at itself and not at the world around it, fails to notice.

# INTRODUCTION

By Isay Weinfeld

I graduated as an architect from Universidade Presbite-riana Mackenzie (Mackenzie Presbyterian University) in 1975, but I never felt like an architect, actually. Perhaps because I feel that defining myself as an architect would restrict my activities to one profession, as if making my ventures into other areas secondary.

Freedom is one of the things I appreciate most in life. Doing what I please, as I please—without feeling tied to a style, a school, or even someone else's expectations. From the start of my career, I have always avoided specializa-tion and sought the challenge of new projects. I believe taking risks is essential. I'd rather fail trying something new than repeat myself doing something I already know I did—and whose outcome I already know.

As an architect, I believe I am, above all, a servant. I have long conversations with the client until I feel that I under-stand what they want and need, whether it's in the way a family lives or the operation of a business. When the client doesn't know exactly what they want, we gradually figure it out together. I then do what they ask of me—but I do it in my own way. It is a long process, from the initial conver-sations to the completion of the project. Every comment, every adjustment the client requests improves the project, bringing it closer to what it should really be.

Over the years, the office has had different structures and dynamics. Today, we are a well-coordinated and well-structured team of more than 50 people with the most diverse ages, backgrounds, experiences, personali-ties, and interests. This highly heterogeneous composition is very rich in the daily work routine as it promotes, in addition to good debates, great exchange and comple-mentarity. We all learn together—about architecture, but also music, cinema, dance, literature, visual arts, fashion. I always encourage especially younger architects to be interested in everything, to seek references, and to build a repertoire beyond architecture. I myself have always been that way, very curious, very eager to go and see things. My greatest references lie outside architecture.

Stanley Kubrick, for example. He made films in the most diverse genres—each film, in itself, brilliant. But the fact that they all share the same identity is particularly admi-rable and incredibly powerful. That's what I would like to see in my work, in my projects, no matter their nature. Identity, not style.

I believe it is this unity that makes the work expressive and conveys strength to people. And that's what inter-ests me, that the project evokes something in people—a memory, a smile, a brief moment of enchantment.

ONE

# HOTELS & RESORTS

# FASANO HOTEL

The Fasano family of São Paulo, the biggest name in Brazilian hospitality for over a century, has parlayed its restaurant expertise into the hotel field. Indeed, the Fasano Hotel in the hip Jardins neighborhood in São Paulo is the fulfillment of a dream by the family to enter the hotel arena. The hotel's design is a collaboration between Isay Weinfeld and Marcio Kogan's Studio MK27.

The project feels as though it has graced the district for generations. With 64 rooms, each offering unique perspectives of the Jardim Europa, a tranquil residential area with tree-lined streets, the hotel affords guests panoramic views. Amenities include a rooftop pool, saunas, a spa, a fitness center, a business center, and Nonno Ruggero, a restaurant serving light meals.

A pivotal design decision was relocating the reception desk to the back of the lobby. Upon entering the main foyer, guests are welcomed with a convivial bar, with the reception desk located discreetly behind it.

On the ground floor, the Baretto bar beckons guests with live jazz and bossa nova; next door, the Fasano Restaurant is a culinary institution known as a Brazilian dining destination. It attracts not just hotel guests but Paulistas themselves, drawn by an Italian menu that celebrates the cuisine of the Fasano family's native country.

**Location:**
São Paulo, Brazil
**Year:**
2003
**Photography:**
Alvaro Povoa
Fernando Guerra
Tuca Reinés

# FAZENDA BOA VISTA

In the countryside of Porto Feliz, just 100 kilometers (52 miles) from São Paulo, the Fazenda Boa Vista complex sprawls across 750 hectares (1,853 acres). This expansive estate includes the Fasano Hotel, private villas, and an array of amenities including a spa, a kids' club, an equestrian center, sports facilities, and two 18-hole golf courses. It is surrounded by lush woodlands and numerous lakes.

Perched atop one of the highest points of the property, the Fasano Hotel commands views of the surrounding lakes, which are especially dramatic at sunset. The distinctive design features a horizontally oriented structure comprising two wings that gracefully curve. One is slightly concave and the other slightly convex and both flank a central core. This core is well-defined between two rustic stone walls, and the interiors abound with Brazilian hardwoods that are found in the structure as well as in the furnishings. At the central lounge, the hallways and rooms converge.

The accommodations are divided between the two wings, with a total of 26 standard rooms (70 m² [753 ft.²] and 11 spacious duplex one-bedroom suites (120 m² [1,292 ft.²]), and one duplex two-bedroom apartment (115 m² [1,238 ft.²]), in addition to one standard accessible room. All rooms have a lake view.

Adjacent to the woods is the spa, a serene retreat characterized by minimalist design. The dramatic, angular structure sheathed in white tile—*branca, branca, branca*. Bright accents of yellow and blue punctuate the space, while expansive windows frame views of the surrounding greenery. Massage rooms, a gym, and wet treatment areas cater to guests seeking rejuvenation and relaxation.

Situated on a gentle slope overlooking the competition track, the equestrian center provides a welcoming space for riders and spectators. The nearby golf clubhouse offers a blend of modern design and verdure. The ground level houses a lounge, bar, restaurant, and offices, with interconnected spaces offering panoramic views of the golf course, accommodated under a single rectangular concrete slab laid on numerous slim stilts. Wooden decked platforms extend from the clubhouse, providing outdoor lounging areas amid the greenery. Below, a heavy concrete block nestled into the slope houses additional facilities, ensuring privacy and functionality for players and staff alike.

The Fazenda Boa Vista complex combines luxury and tranquility. Guests enjoy a complex of many uses amid the natural beauty and idyllic countryside of Porto Feliz.

**Location:**
Porto Feliz, Brazil
**Year:**
2011
**Photography:**
Fernando Guerra
Nelson Kon

## THE HOTEL

## THE SPA

# THE EQUESTRIAN CENTER

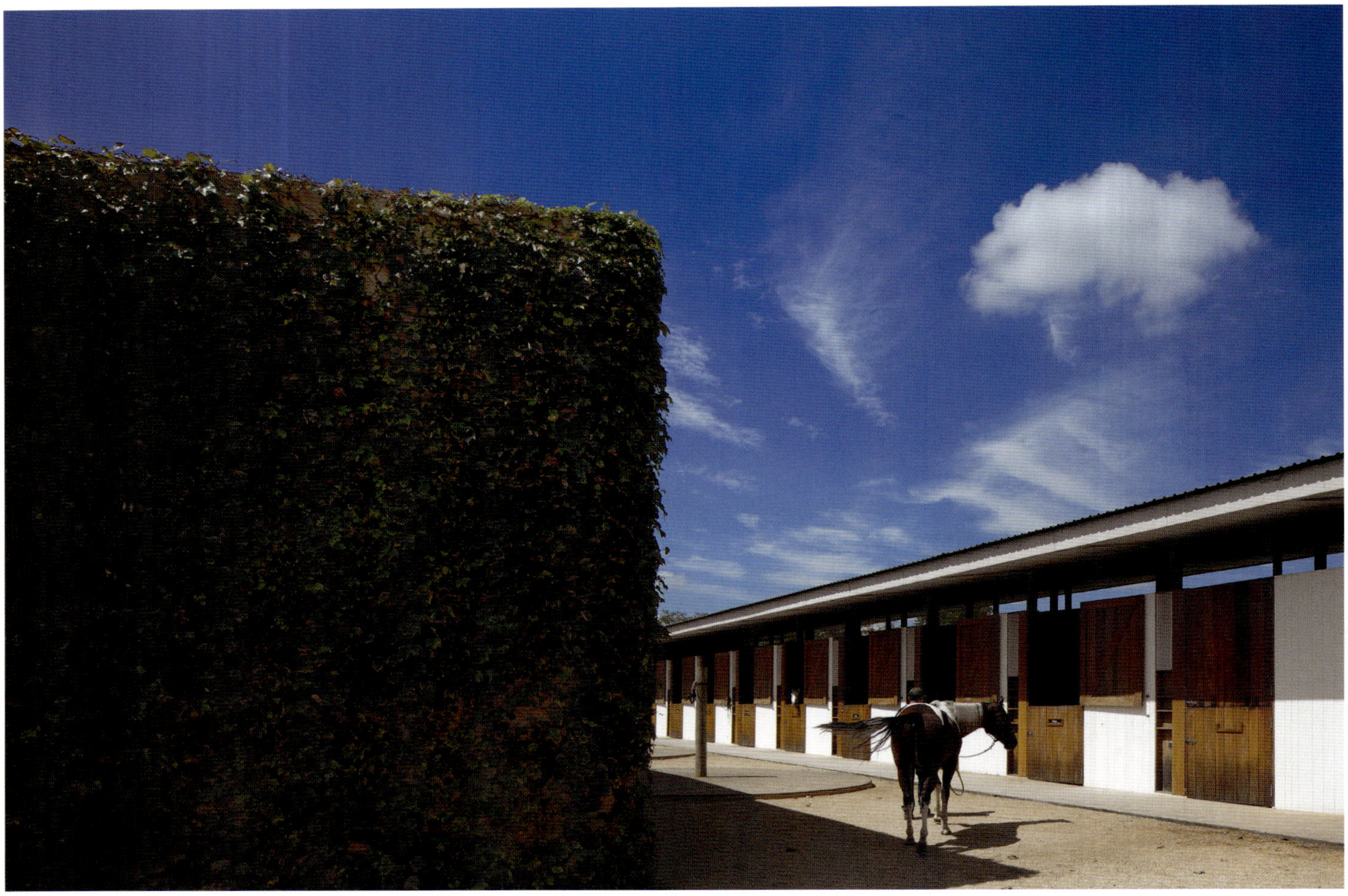

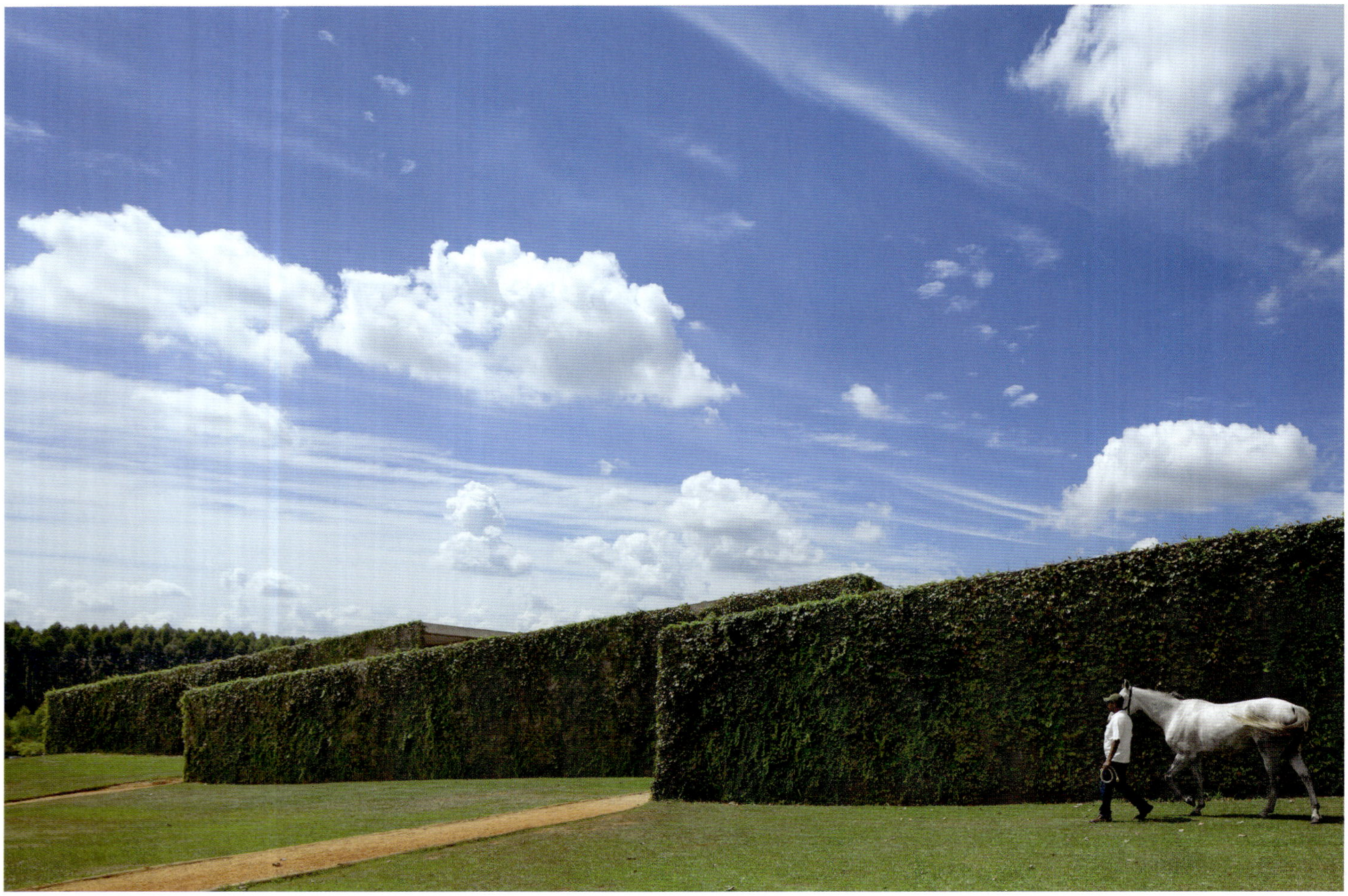

## THE GOLF CLUBHOUSE

FAZENDA BOA VISTA

# SQUARE NINE HOTEL

Square Nine Hotel is in Belgrade's historic quarter, directly facing Students' Square (Studentski Trg). It is a strikingly modern design that seamlessly integrates with the surrounding buildings, respecting their scales, rhythms, and color palettes.

Upon entering, guests are greeted by expansive interconnected spaces, including the lobby, restaurant, and a piazza. Descending to the basement level reveals a tranquil oasis featuring a swimming pool illuminated by a cascade of natural light. A gym, spa, and sauna are nearby. Meanwhile, on the top floor a bar offers picturesque views of the bustling square below.

The hotel offers three room categories spread across five levels, comprising 32 or 47 m² (345 or 505 ft.²) double rooms and spacious 90 m² (969 ft.²) suites, totaling 45 units. Each floor boasts a unique hall adjacent to the lifts, adorned with unexpected pieces of furniture that add character to the space.

Premium materials such as wood, stone, and leather combine with a carefully curated selection of vintage furniture by Scandinavian and North American designers of the 1930s through the 1960s. A mid-century vibe pervades the entire complex.

**Location:**
Belgrade, Serbia
**Year:**
2011
**Photography:**
Matthieu Salvaing

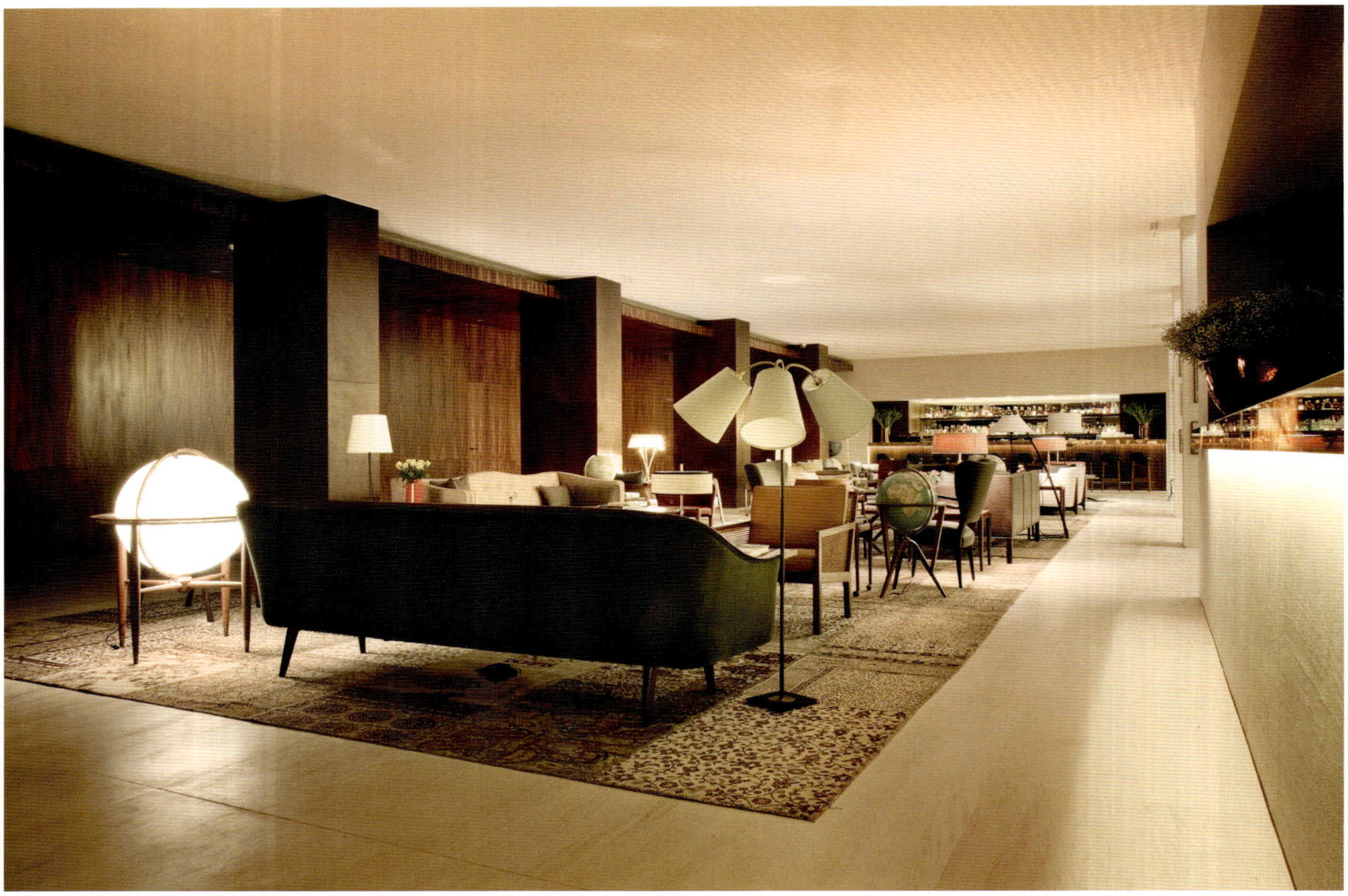

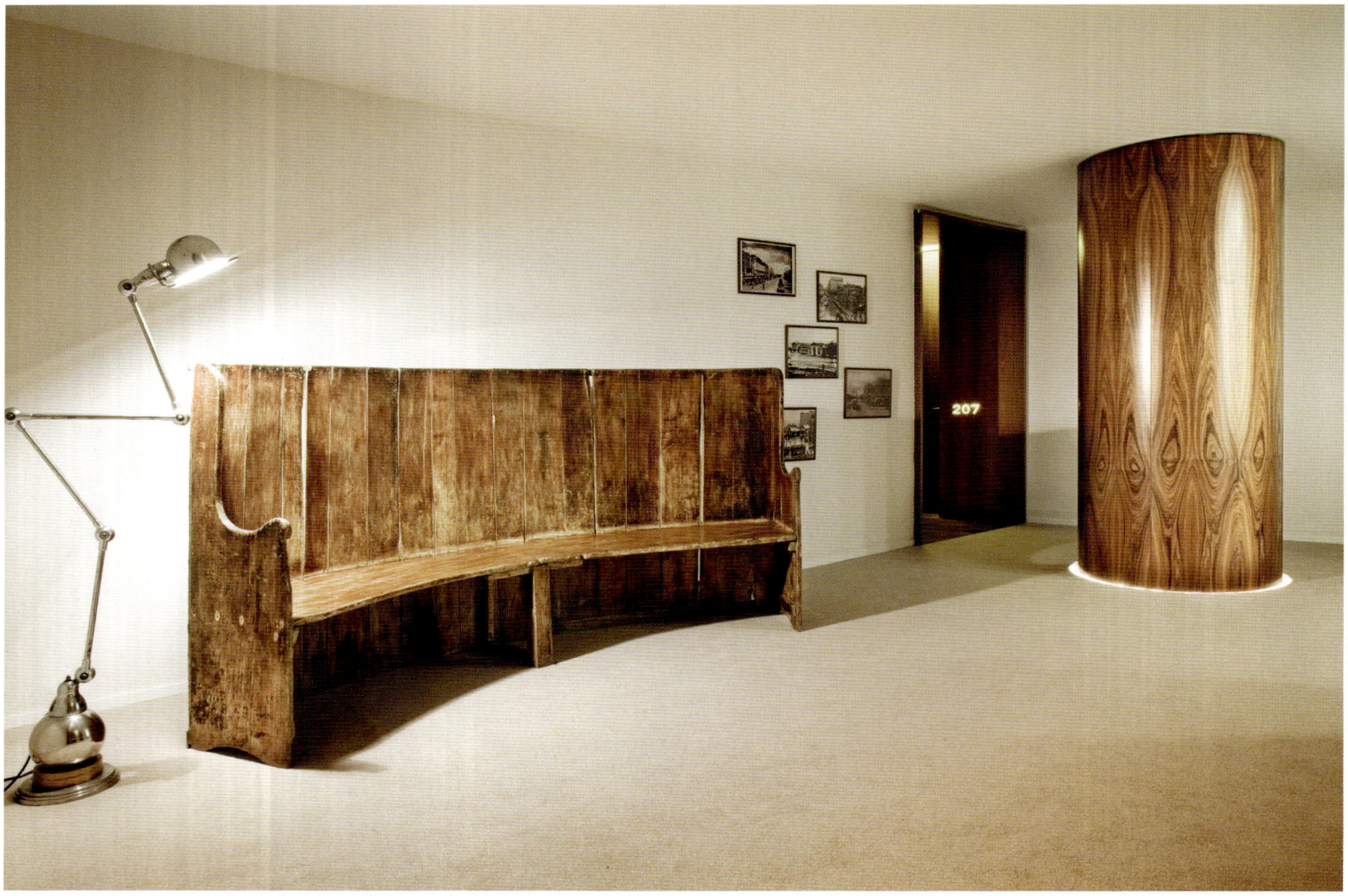
207

# FASANO LAS PIEDRAS

Punta del Este, Uruguay, is a resort destination for the South American and European elite. The Fasano Las Piedras complex spans 480 hectares (1.186 acres) of awe-inspiring landscape characterized by arid, rocky terrain and sparse vegetation. Las Piedras seamlessly integrates private homes, hotel bungalows, and a range of amenities including a spa, equestrian center, and golf and polo fields, along a 3-kilometer (1.86-mile) stretch of beach called Arroyo Maldonado.

Wood and concrete—that's the prevailing first impression of Las Piedras. To honor the natural beauty of the surroundings, meticulous planning went into the layout of the complex. Units were strategically scattered across the land, mirroring the natural formations of the rocks in a seamless integration with the landscape.

The Fasano Las Piedras spa is housed in a single-story concrete structure. Rooms encircle an open indoor garden, suffusing the space with a tranquil ambience accentuated by natural light filtering through windows and skylights. The spa offers treatment rooms, dry and wet saunas, a swimming pool, relaxation areas, and a private suite.

Positioned strategically to offer sweeping views, the swimming pool sits atop a high point of the land, nestled within a natural depression in the rocks. Adjacent to the pool, a weathering steel container houses changing rooms, a bar, and a lounge.

When architects discovered rustic buildings crafted from local rocks on the property, preservation became paramount. The former owner's home and studio now house the hotel reception area, the Las Piedras Restaurant, and the Fasano Restaurant. This thoughtful integration of existing structures further enhances the charm and character of Fasano Las Piedras, where guests are immersed in the beauty of Punta del Este.

**Location:**
Punta Del Este, Uruguay
**Year:**
2012
**Photography:**
Fernando Guerra
Tuca Reinés
Luisa Sigulem

## THE SPA

# THE HOTEL

## THE SWIMMING POOL BAR

## THE LOUNGE

## FASANO RESTAURANT

## RECEPTION AND LAS PIEDRAS RESTAURANT

# B HOTEL

Brasília, Brazil's capital city, is loved and hated in equal measure. No one is indifferent in his or her opinion of this audacious, mid-century planned city.

B Hotel boasts a prime location at the heart of Brasília's Northern Hotel Sector, situated directly on the bustling Eixo Monumental amid the city's iconic government buildings, monuments, and memorials. Positioned on a unique lot that delineates the boundary between towering high-rise hotels and a more verdant, low-density area, the hotel offers a captivating blend of urban vibrancy and rural tranquility.

Designed as a business-oriented establishment, B Hotel caters primarily to visitors seeking accommodation for events and meetings at government agencies, embassies, and local companies, particularly during the week. Adhering to local regulations, the hotel's architecture harmonizes with its surroundings, featuring a wide rectangular prism (15 x 60 m [49 x 196 ft.], rising 55 meters (180 feet) high, with a horizontal base (60 x 60 m [196 x 196 ft.]) and 6 meters (19.6 feet) in height at the second floor. This base elegantly interfaces with neighboring structures while appearing to levitate above the ground floor on stilts.

The main tower hosts hotel rooms and suites across 15 floors, offering panoramic views of the city from its rooftop bar and pool area. Leveraging a permitted cantilever (2 m [6.5 ft.]) at 70 percent of the façade, each room features strategically positioned windows (2 x 2 m [6.5 x 6.5 ft.]), creating a visually dynamic façade characterized by intriguing shadows and lending personality to the building.

Upon arrival on the ground floor, guests are welcomed by a reception lobby, bar, and restaurant, fostering an inviting and lively atmosphere. The second floor houses versatile event spaces, including a ballroom and smaller meeting rooms, accessible either through the hotel lobby or via a separate entrance from the stilts below.

"*Brasilia – The City of the Future!*" is a modernist architectural wonderland, and B Hotel places guests right in the midst of it all.

**Location:**
Brasilia, Brazil
**Year:**
2018
**Photography:**
Fernando Guerra

# FASANO TRANCOSO HOTEL

Nestled along the shores of Itapororoca Beach in Bahia, in northeast Brazil, the Fasano Trancoso Hotel occupies a sprawling lot extending over 500 meters (1,640 feet) along the beach.

The hotel is meticulously organized. This streamlines the property operations to ensure guest privacy and optimize ocean vistas. A tranquil stream meanders across the property. Support, administrative, and leisure facilities are thoughtfully positioned along the hotel's perimeter, while the central area is dedicated exclusively to the bungalows. The residential units are strategically situated on one side of the stream, with the hotel units nestled on the opposite side, all interconnected by lush bromeliads, heliconias, and native coconut trees. This abundant vegetation ensures privacy among units and provides shade in the unforgiving tropical climate.

A wooden deck stretches along the beach and is adjacent to five swimming pools. A beach club anchors one end of the deck; at the other extreme there is a spa that offers views of the ocean and the surrounding forest.

The Fasano Trancoso Hotel uses natural and rustic materials, including mortar, adobe, wood, and thatch, in a soft, light palette. This is in keeping with the Fasano family's hotel brand, which is all about daring architecture and an absence of ostentation.

**Location:**
Trancoso, Brazil
**Year:**
2022
**Photography:**
Fernando Guerra

FASANO TRANCCSO HOTEL

# FASANO SALVADOR HOTEL

The Fasano Salvador Hotel occupies an Art Deco building built in the 1920s as the headquarters of the newspaper *A Tarde*, in the historic center of Salvador, in the state of Bahia, in the northeast of Brazil.

The building's façade is protected by preservation codes. Nonetheless, designers were free to rearrange the interior layout, respecting the structure and original elements of the building—doors, wall and ceiling ornaments, and the hall floor, exquisitely laid in marble *cabochon*.

With 70 rooms spread over 11 floors, the hotel also has a lobby, restaurant, spa, business center, and a rooftop pool.

The choice of finishes was largely a symbolic nod to local history and culture. Thus, dark wood panels pay homage to the famous *Jacaranda-da-Bahia*, now unfortunately extinct; *Azul-Bahia* granite covers the pool, giving it a deep blue, almost as if it extended to the sea that can be seen in front of it; and, finally, linens and laces, so well-known in local craftsmanship, complete the palette of materials that give the spaces a cozy and relaxed atmosphere within the sophistication that distinguishes the Fasano brand.

**Location:**
Salvador, Brazil
**Year:**
2010
**Photography:**
Fernando Guerra

TWO

# BARS & RESTAURANTS

# FASANO RESTAURANT SÃO PAULO

The Fasano Restaurant São Paulo could be a set for a James Bond thriller, circa 1960. The design rejuvenates Brazil's most cherished culinary brand. Located within the Fasano Hotel, the restaurant has a stylish bar, a spacious dining room with 20 tables (seating 80 patrons), a private function room accommodating 26, a curated wine cellar, and essential facilities spread across two levels and mezzanines.

Access to the restaurant is seamlessly integrated with the hotel lobby. A welcoming low-ceilinged bar leads to the main dining area, which has a wide layout with a double-height ceiling and a retractable glass roof, creating a luminous and inviting atmosphere.

The private function room and cellar are strategically placed on mezzanines at opposite ends of the dining space, offering intimate settings for special occasions and wine enthusiasts. The kitchen and supporting facilities are discreetly located on the underground level, ensuring efficient service without disrupting patrons' dining experience.

In the space, one can almost hear: "The name is Bond. James Bond."

**Location:**
São Paulo, Brazil
**Year:**
2003
**Photography:**
Fernando Guerra
Tuca Reinés
Alvaro Povoa

FASANO RESTAURANT SÃO PAULO

# BAR NÚMERO

Bar Número was built on a very narrow and long strip of land in the Jardins area of São Paulo. A walkway runs from the street through a hallway—a tunnel fully covered in mirrors—leading to the main hall.

At the entrance, the ceiling is low and the view of the cascading hall is unimpeded. Progressing towards the back, the ceiling height gradually increases. Descending levels feature comfortable lounging areas under a ceiling that extends on a continually rising surface.

The low and indirect lighting throughout lends the ambiance a pleasant and cozy atmosphere, perfect for a relaxing drink at the end of the day, accompanied by friends and the sound of good music.

A room reserved for private functions occupies the lower floor. It has couches placed along the central axis of the room, built-in overhead lighting, and walls completely covered by antique posters or poster fragments.

The façade is covered in wooden blocks made from laser-cut marine plywood coated in resin, referencing the movable blocks used in typography.

**Location:**
São Paulo, Brazil
**Year:**
2010
**Photography:**
Leonardo Finotti

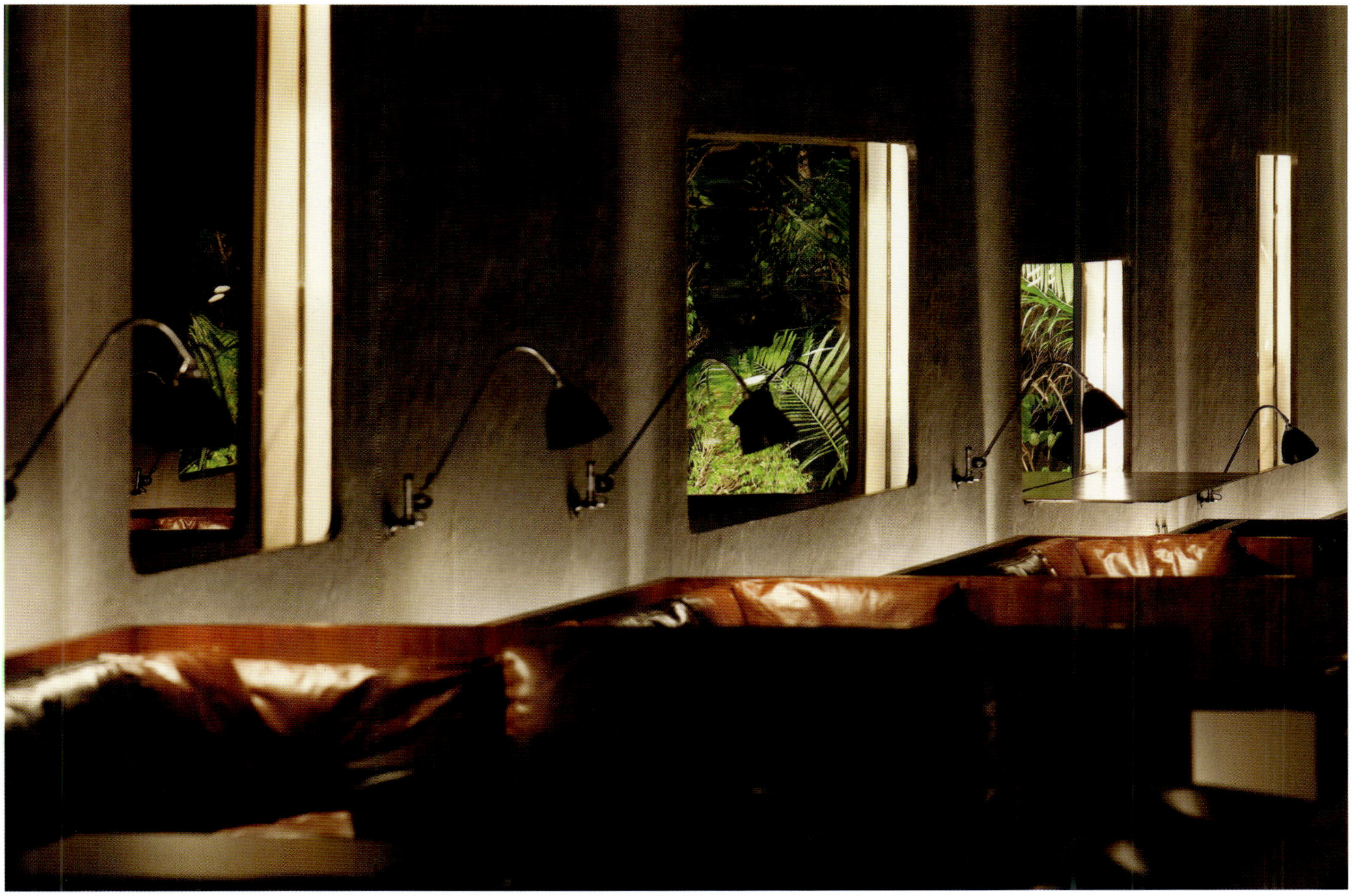

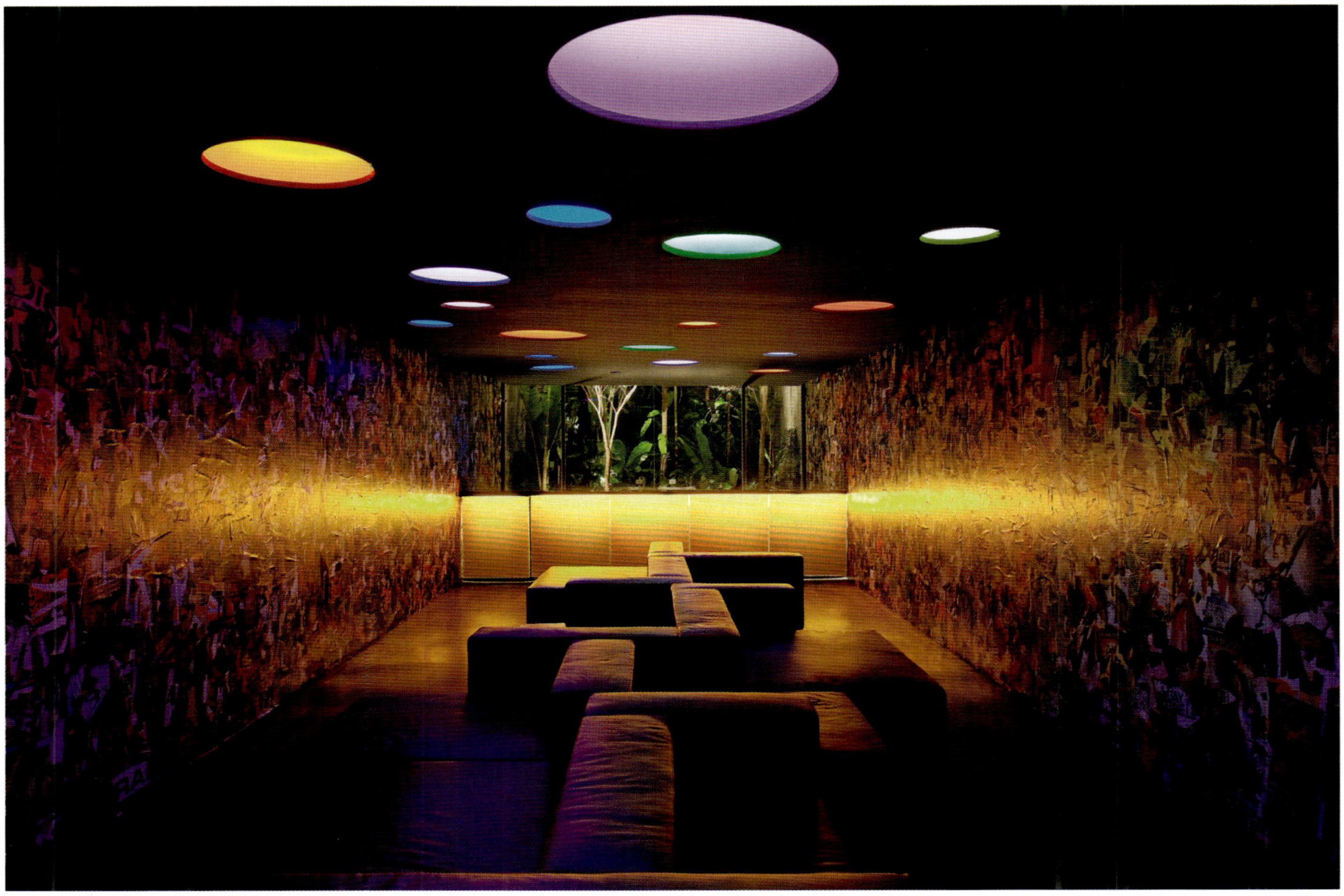

# GREEN SPOT RESTAURANT

Green Spot Restaurant lies within Barcelona's historic Ciutat Vella, "Old Town," where the winding streets of Barri Gòtic merge with the structured layout of Barceloneta, a neighborhood created in the 18th century from land reclaimed from the sea.

Occupying a rectangular plot that spans the entire block, the building seamlessly integrates the restaurant at street level with four floors of apartment units above.

At ground level, the foyer to the residential section gracefully transitions from the bustling pedestrian street to a tranquil courtyard nestled within the heart of the building. This thoughtful design maximizes commercial space, with two narrow strips flanking the central courtyard designated for technical areas, while a spacious dining room occupies the opposite end, spanning the width of the plot.

The dining area, overlooking Pas de Sota Muralla, is captivating. Its striking architectural features—a grid of solid columns and a vaulted ceiling—not only add character but also create private pockets within the space.

The lush courtyard, adorned with vegetation, floods the interior with natural light, illuminating every corner of the restaurant. Serving as a serene focal point, it connects the dining room to adjacent technical and supporting areas—the kitchen on one side, washrooms and storage areas on the other. Each is conveniently accessible from the street.

Green Spot Restaurant offers easy access to Barcelona destinations like La Rambla and architect Antoni Gaudí's Basílica de la Sagrada Família. Like the surrounding region, Barcelona is fiercely independent but always welcoming to visitors.

**Location:**
Barcelona, Spain
**Year:**
2016
**Photography:**
Iñigo Bujedo Aguirre

# FASANO RESTAURANT NY

Patterned after the famed Four Seasons Restaurant in the adjacent Seagram Building in midtown Manhattan, Fasano Restaurant New York is on the ground floor of 280 Park Avenue, a 1960s-era office building. Fasano Restaurant's mid-century ambience recalls the golden age of the "young executive," a dashing figure celebrated in movies and on American television in the 1950s and 1960s.

The foyer, clad in Radica—a Brazilian quartz with iron oxides—creates a seamless transition from the street to the restaurant's interior. The first dining room features wood, sandstone, and bronze-colored mirrors. Combined with the soft light filtering through the casement behind the bar, this creates a cozy and relaxed atmosphere. Benches set in mirrored booths along the side walls are complemented by an exclusive reissue of chairs designed by Edward Wormley, a mid-century American furniture designer.

A secondary hall, positioned next to the wine cellar, leads to tables on the terrace overlooking 49th Street, while a passage opposite the bar—raised by a few steps—leads to the second dining room. In the second, larger room, natural materials and neutral colors still prevail. However, the inclusion of wall-to-wall carpeting, delicate light fixtures on the pillars, and a layout with more spacious tables separated by wicker screens imbue the room with a more formal and sophisticated atmosphere.

The long walkway connecting the two rooms is adorned with brass plates and provides access to a private function room seating 22, as well as to Baretto, a live music bar. Both spaces feature independent access and dedicated service structures. Throughout the restaurant there is a carefully curated collection of photographs, objects, and antiques.

*Mad Men*, anyone? Take the 11:45 a.m. to Grand Central and enjoy lunch at this lively spot.

**Location:**
New York, United States
**Year:**
2022
**Photography:**
Fernando Guerra
Eric Mesker

# LE PAVILLON

In the heart of midtown Manhattan, Le Pavillon is a spacious 1,000 m² (3,281 ft.²) dining sanctuary. It is located within One Vanderbilt, a new mixed-use office/residential/commercial tower completed in 2020. Located on the second level, Le Pavillon is named after the illustrious New York eatery founded by Henri Soulé in 1941.

Under the guidance of Chef Daniel Boulud, Le Pavillon's menu centers around seafood. The restaurant's expansive dining room accommodates 120 diners; an adjacent 46-seat bar/lounge offers views of surrounding landmarks like Grand Central Terminal and the Chrysler Building.

Unexpected design touches abound—a wall that seems fashioned out of bamboo; hanging chandeliers of hand-blown glass; varying ceiling heights that play with notions of enclosure and release; walkways that meander through greenery fashioned as an indoor park. The semi-private Garden Table is set in a grove of olive trees.

In sum, Le *nouveau* Pavillon lives up to the reputation of its vaunted namesake.

**Location:**
New York, United States
**Year:**
2021
**Photography:**
Fernando Guerra

# MOCOTÓ RESTAURANT

Mocotó Restaurant, in the Knightsbridge section of London, is distributed over two floors.

The lower level serves traditional Brazilian dishes, while the upper floor is a reinterpretation of the traditional *boteco*, the Brazilian street bar that generally serves "cachaça" and other typical finger foods in a very casual and relaxed atmosphere.

At the Mocotó bar, the chairs are typical of Brazilian pubs and the tables were designed especially for the project. The chairs are original pieces made of jacaranda, a subtropical wood native to south-central South America that was popularized in the 1950s by Brazilian designer Sérgio Rodrigues.

Mocotó recalls Brazil's 1950s and 1960s heyday—vibrant, full of optimism, and uniquely *brasileiro*.

**Location:**
London, United Kingdom
**Year:**
2007
**Photography:**
Leonardo Finotti

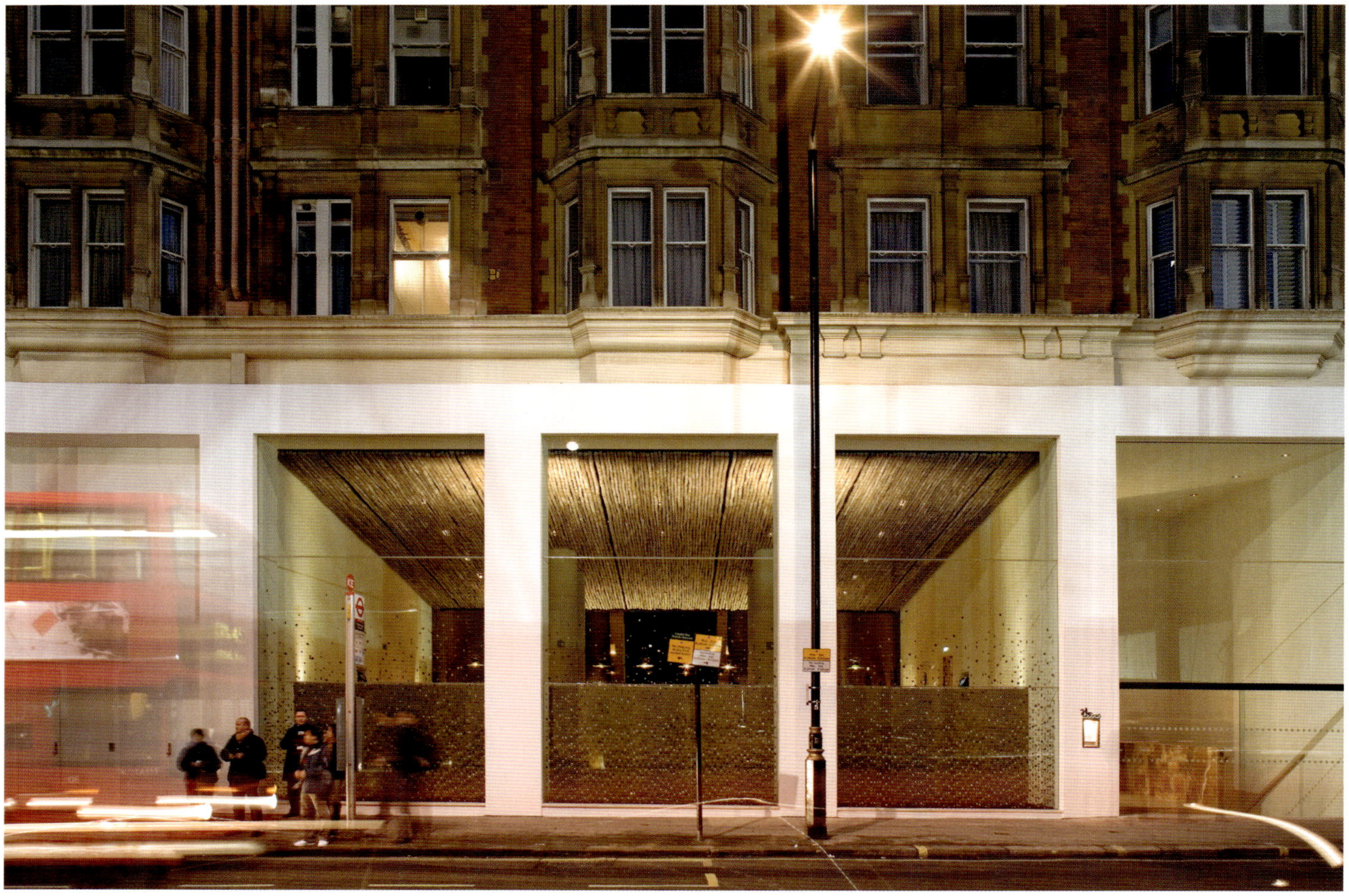

TRANSDEV
HIGH AND
MIGHTY
FASHI

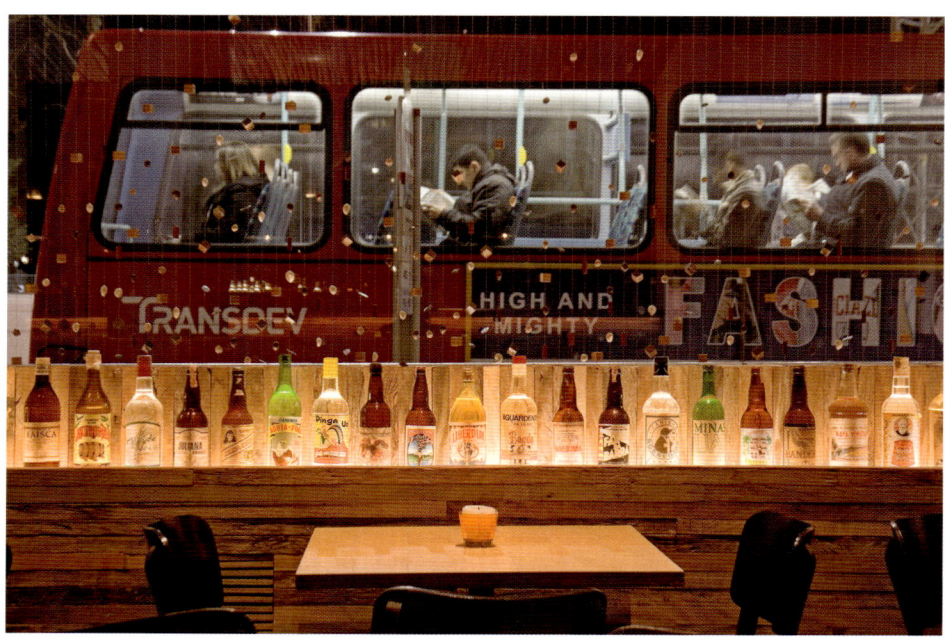

THREE

# SHOPS & CULTURAL CENTER

# FORUM

Forum is a top name in Brazilian fashion, epitomizing style with an authentic Brazilian *espírito*. The goal for the new flagship store in São Paulo was to capture the essence of the brand, employing contemporary aesthetics while celebrating Brazil's rich cultural heritage through shape, color, and materials.

The store boasts distinct entrances—one to a men's fashion section and one to a women's section. On the lower floor there is a collection of sportswear; the upper level contains an array of evening wear and haute couture.

At the heart of the space the two wings converge. A stairway adorned with red glass mosaic tiles leads to a mezzanine and a bar, the latter crafted from taipa—a traditional Brazilian building material made of clay and dried vines. It evokes the rustic allure of northeastern Brazil.

Throughout, elements of Brazilian craftsmanship add depth and character. White rag rugs, reminiscent of traditional Brazilian handicraft, imbue the space with warmth and texture. There are signature armchairs designed by Brazilian visionaries from the 1950s; subtle details like straw accents on door handles and solid treetrunk barstools add whimsy.

These elements contrast with the store's clean lines and meticulously organized spaces. It is a retail environment with a Brazilian soul—*uma alma brasileira*.

**Location:**
São Paulo, Brazil
**Year:**
2000
**Photography:**
Tuca Reinés
Fernando Guerra

# LIVRARIA DA VILA

Livraria da Vila is street-front bookstore in São Paulo occupying a narrow plot of land.

The design prioritizes customer comfort and engagement. Under indirect lighting, extensive shelves of books, meticulously arranged and curated, stretch from floor to ceiling. The abundance of books creates an inviting ambience reminiscent of a cozy used bookstore. Shoppers are encouraged to peruse the shelves, browse through pages, or relax on couches and armchairs scattered across multiple levels.

The basement level is dedicated to children. A small adjacent auditorium hosts lectures and author book signings.

Recognizing the need for an open plan, architects undertook significant structural modifications, including the integration of metal components to relocate pillars and reinforce the foundation.

Design elements, such as the pivoting window-shelf-doors and the interconnected voids between floors, beckon customers to explore. Livraria da Vila is a creative environment that combines functionality and aesthetics. It is conceived by book lovers for book lovers.

**Location:**
São Paulo, Brazil
**Year:**
2007
**Photography:**
Leonardo Finotti

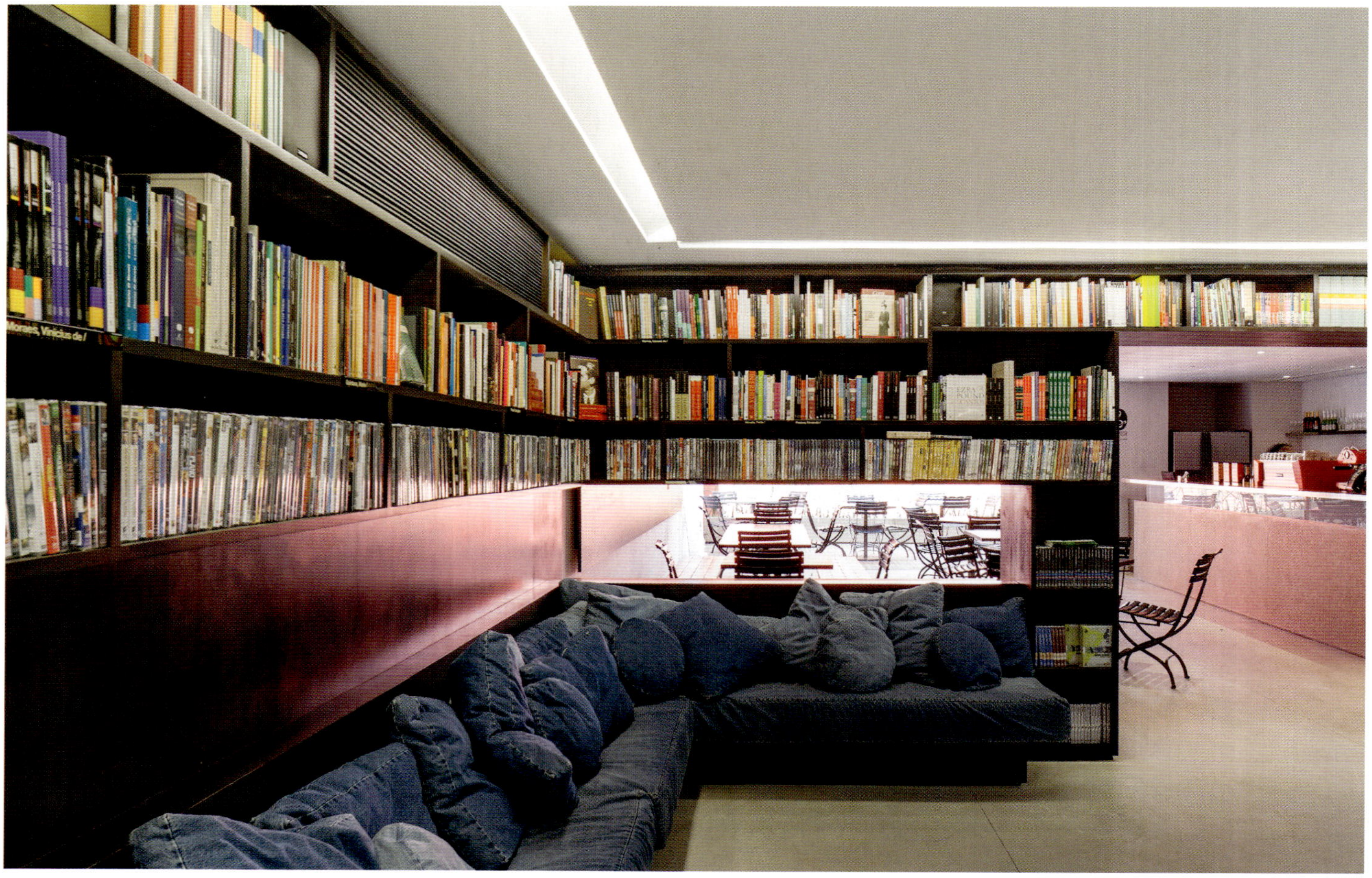

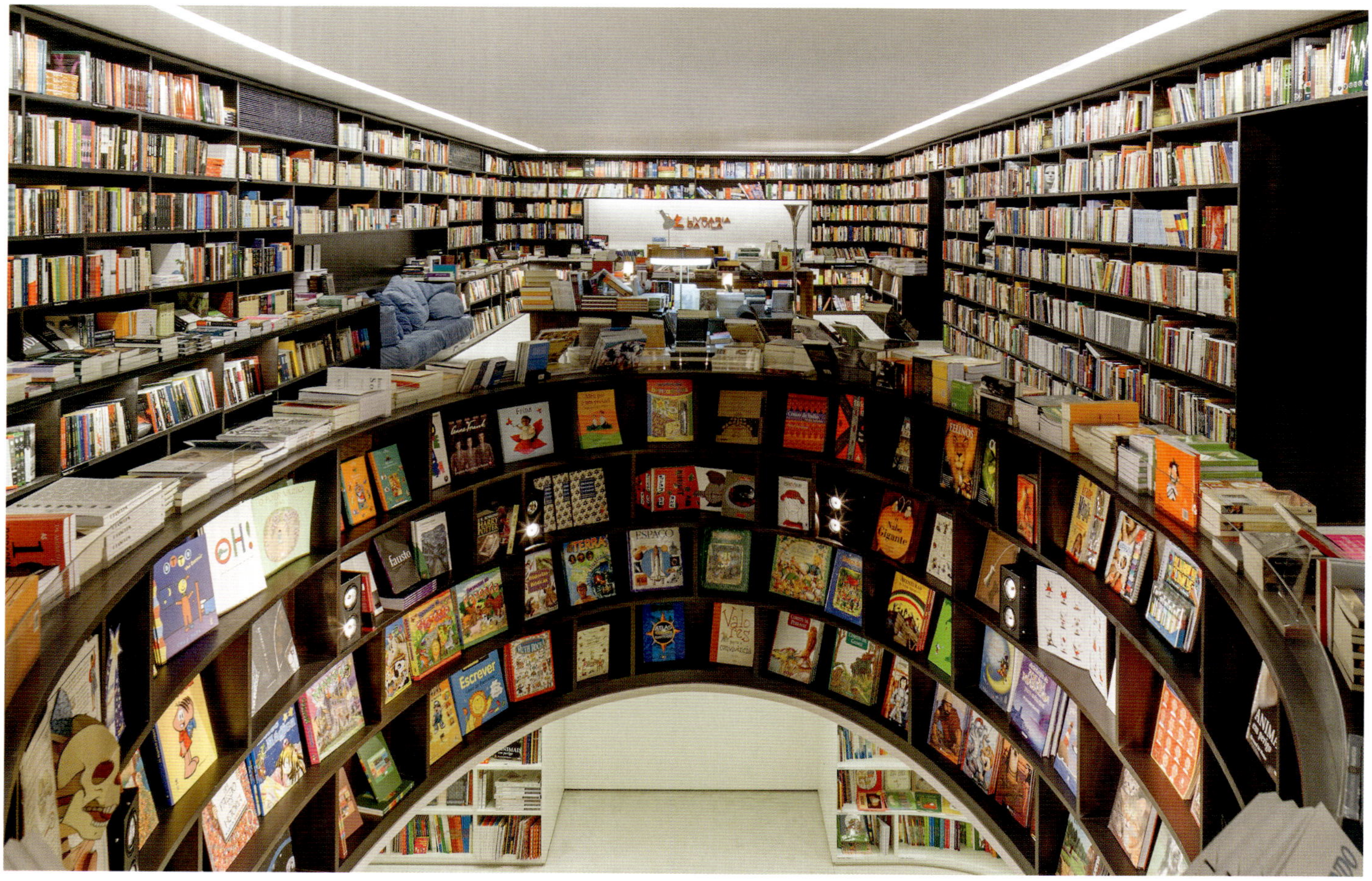

# LIVRARIA DA VILA |
# CIDADE JARDIM MALL

Located in Cidade Jardim Mall in São Paulo, this Livraria da Vila speaks to the role design plays in enhancing a product, its presentation, and ultimately its sales. This project focused on creating solutions that prioritize customer comfort and engagement with products.

Visitors are welcomed into the store through pivoting window-shelf-doors on the ground floor. A staircase to the right leads to a mezzanine that runs along the perimeter of the lower hall, connecting to three glazed volumes that extend over the expansive central void. These volumes house an auditorium for courses and lectures; a section dedicated to classical music and jazz CDs; and a space reserved for author book signings and book launch events.

Spanning 2,300 m$^2$ (24,760 ft.$^2$) across two levels, the store offers a range of environments. Customers can browse and read in comfortable couches or easy chairs. Children have their own dedicated space, complete with a small theater designed for storytelling sessions. Meanwhile, families and groups can gather in the coffee house, featuring a double-height ceiling and fully glazed walls. It is a vibrant atmosphere conducive to lively conversations.

In addition to the U-shaped staircase at the entrance, an elevator, and an additional staircase aid vertical circulation. Livraria da Vila Cidade Jardim Mall invites customers to immerse themselves in a book-browsing experience; every corner beckons readers to explore and discover.

**Location:**
São Paulo, Brazil
**Year:**
2008
**Photography:**
Leonardo Finotti

Robert Schumann,
Nat King Cole,
Henry Purcell,
Duke Ellington,
Ella Fitzgerald

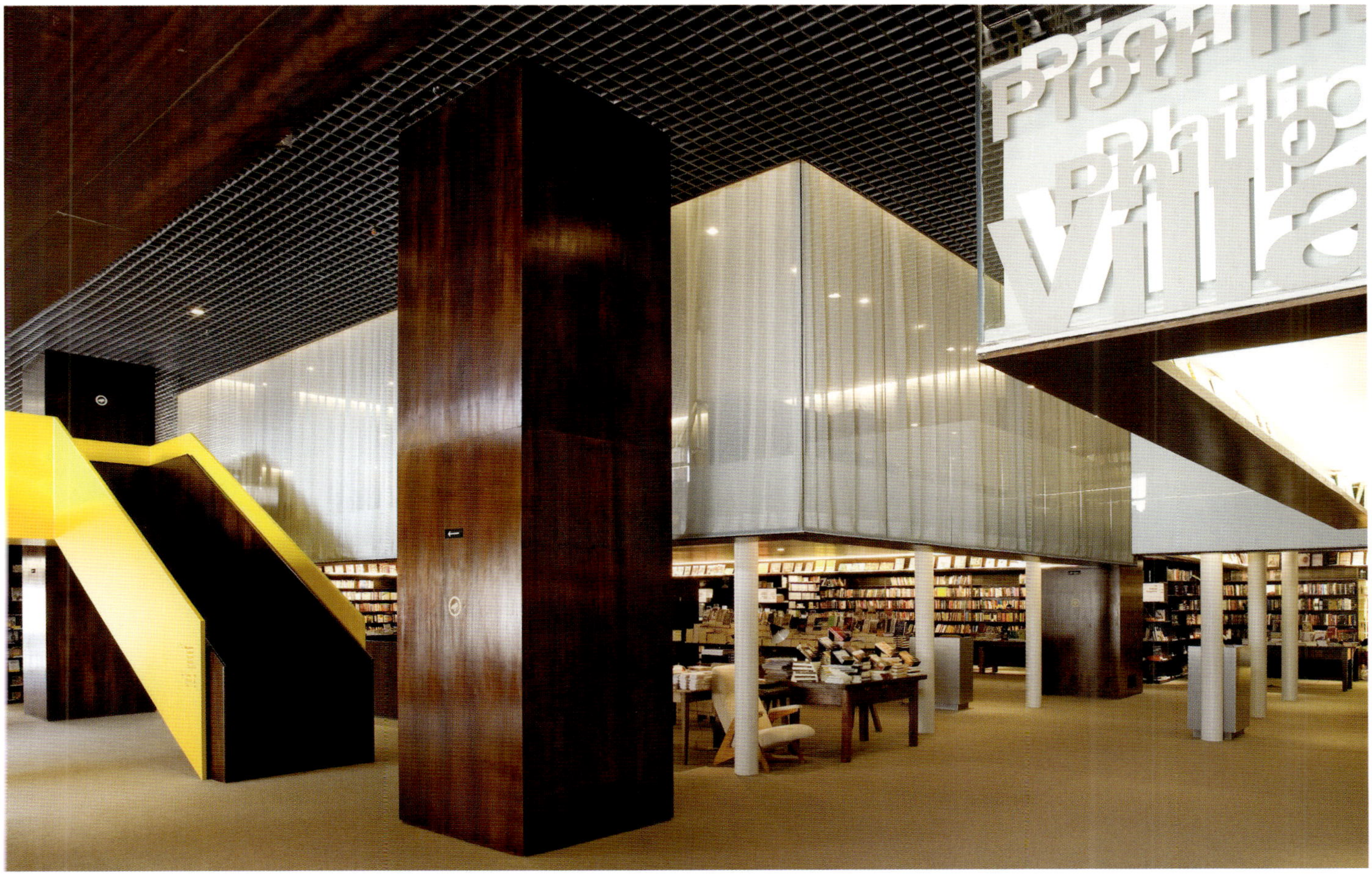
Villa

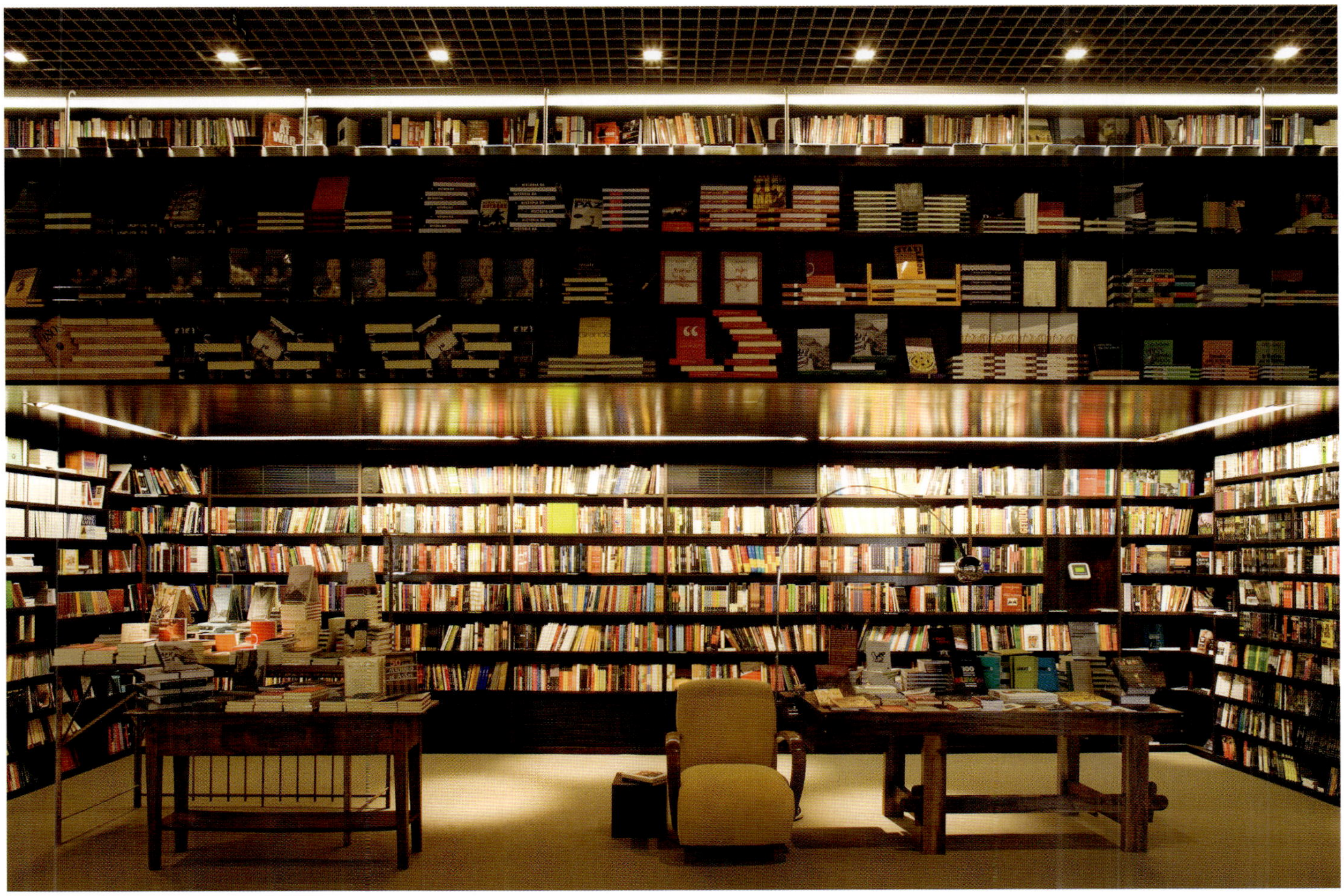

# HAVAIANAS

Since their creation in 1962, inspired by the traditional Japanese "zori" slippers made of rice straw, Havaianas sandals have undergone a remarkable transformation from humble rubber flip-flops to global fashion symbols of style and comfort.

At the store on Rua Oscar Freire, São Paulo, one of the world's most prestigious retail addresses, offering products at the low end of the price range was both a challenge and an opportunity for the brand. This flagship store marks Havaianas' inaugural retail presence in Brazil, and the goal was to capture the essence of the brand: freshness, informality, comfort, ease, well-being, and an *essência brasileira*.

The store emanates an informal vibe. Indeed it resembles an open square integrated into the sidewalk. Dispensing with traditional doors and window displays, the façade features lush greenery and abundant natural light. There is a metal grid alternating glass and wooden elements for ventilation and irrigation.

Internally, the store is organized into levels: the street level hosts a cozy terrace and a mezzanine that offers a bird's-eye view of the activity below. The main floor has double-height ceilings and distinct zones. A street market stand pays tribute to the sandals' humble origins and a container showcases "export" models previously unavailable in Brazil. Finally a transparent cylinder highlights new product offerings and a high-tech cube narrates the brand's 60-plus year journey.

Additionally, a dedicated area offers customization services and displays for the children's product line. Towards the rear, a half-raised level features a tranquil garden exclusively for staff use, while the underground area accommodates offices and storage.

**Location:**
São Paulo, Brazil
**Year:**
2009
**Photography:**
Nelson Kon

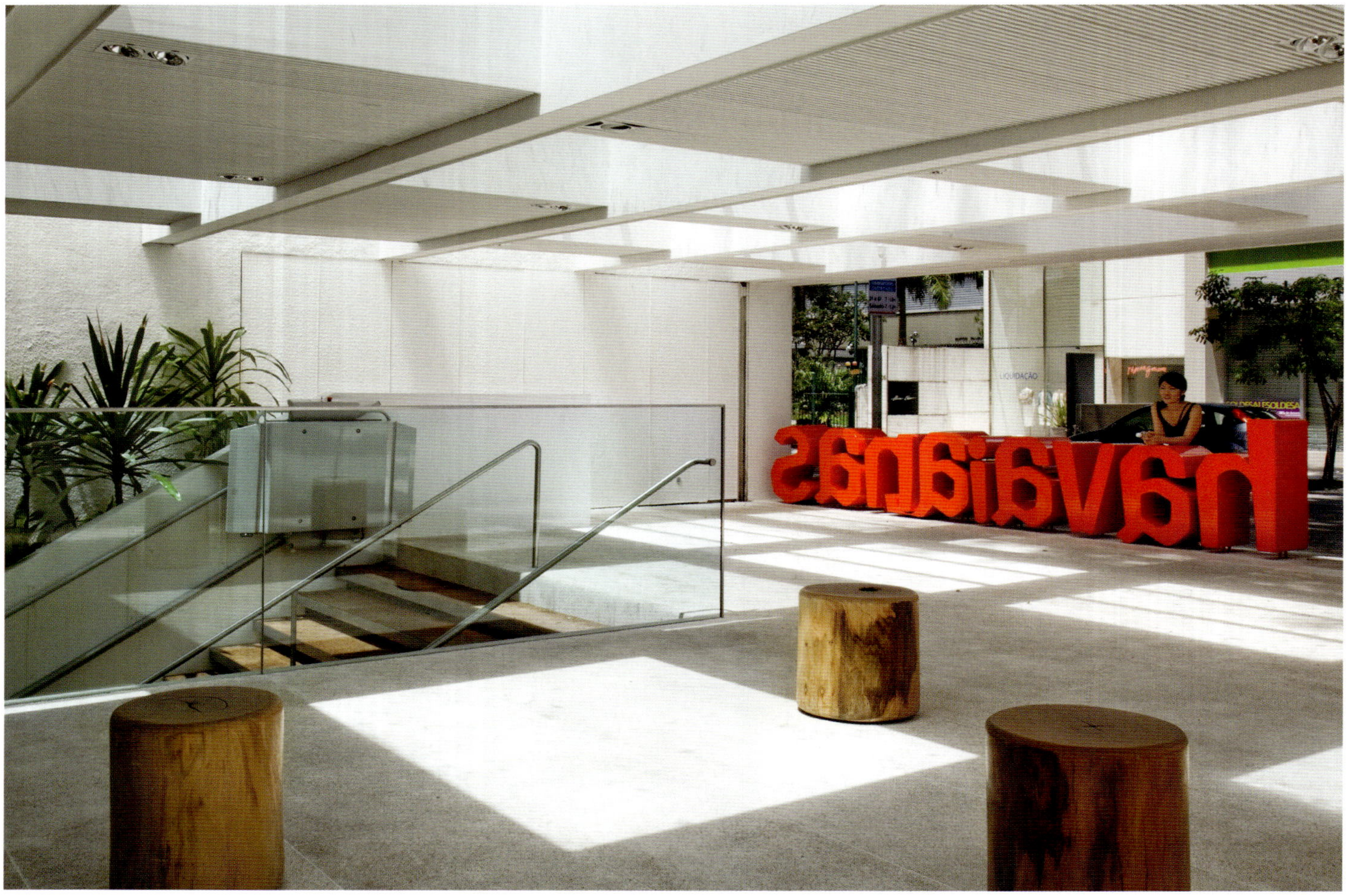

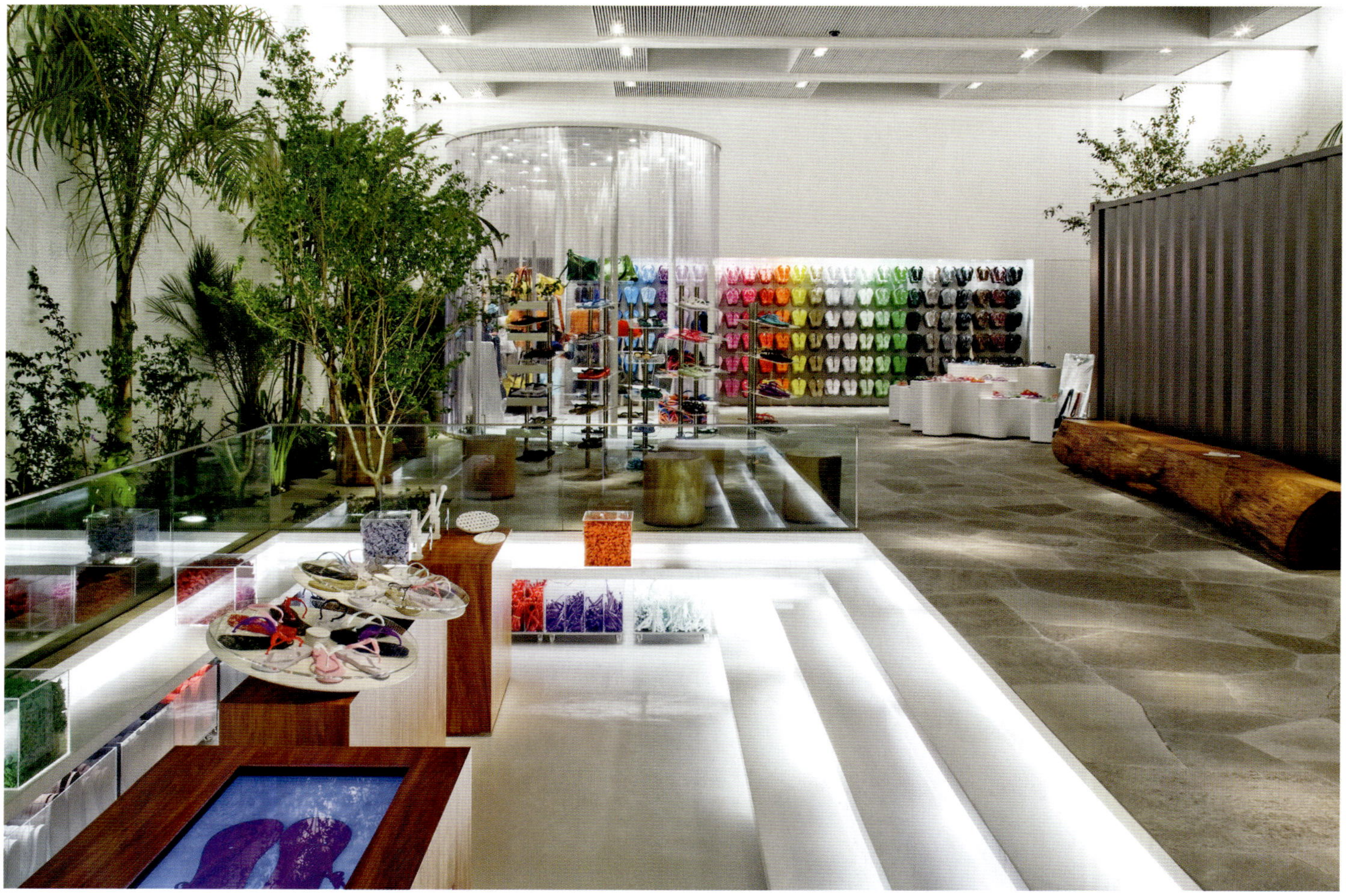

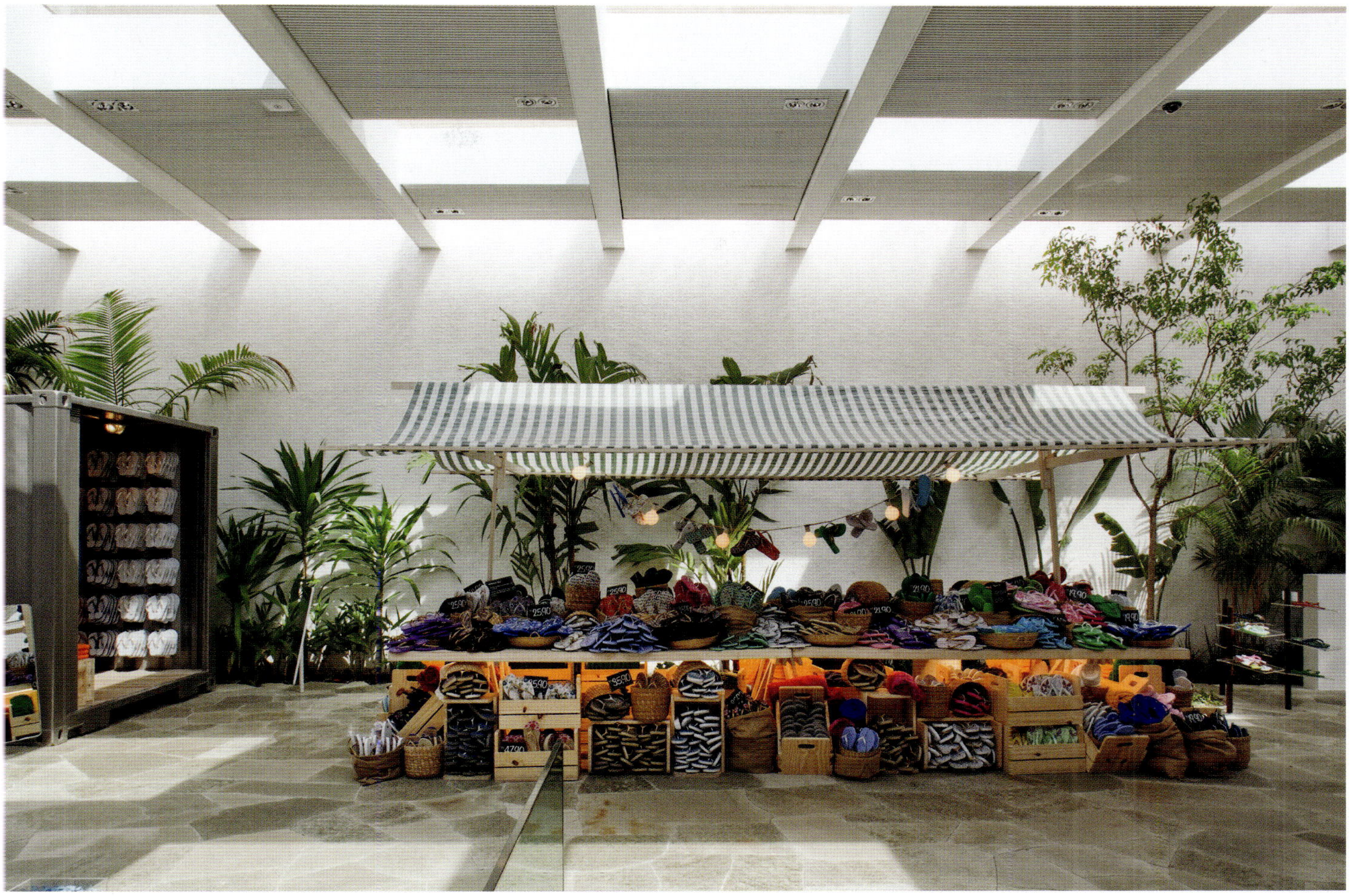

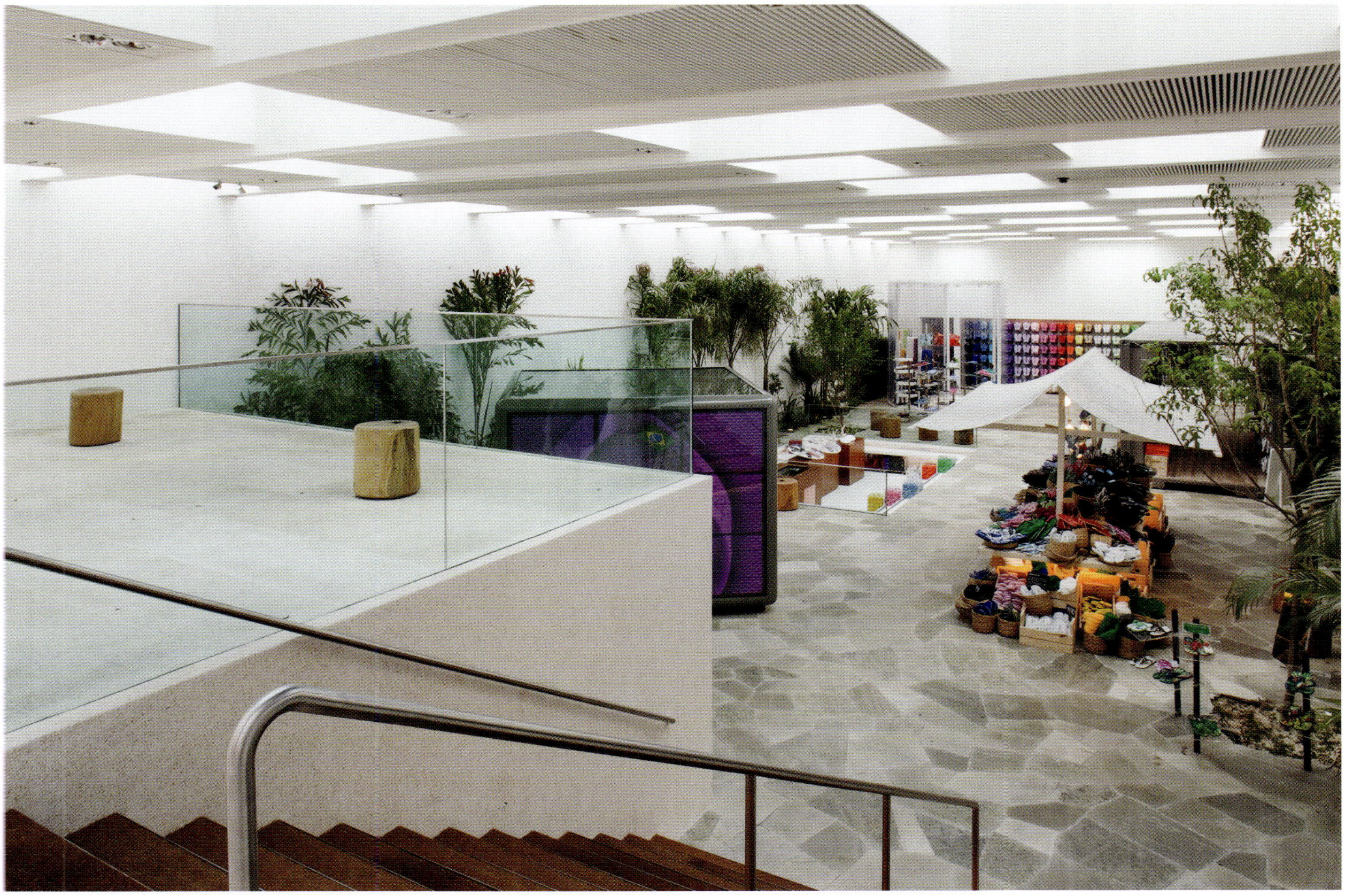

# LIVRARIA DA VILA |
# JK IGUATEMI MALL

The Livraria da Vila store at JK Iguatemi Mall in greater
São Paulo occupies a rectangular 1,700 m² (18,300 ft.²)
space adorned with sturdy square pillars and featuring
ceilings that are 4.5 meters (14.7 feet) high. The store's
sinuous shelving is quintessentially Brazilian—not unlike
the curves in an Oscar Niemeyer building.

The store offers a picturesque vista through a large
window overlooking a nearby park. The design strategy
focused on centralizing supporting activities, such as
the café, children's section, and a small auditorium on
the mezzanine, to the sides of the rectangle. This layout
fosters a spacious square room dedicated to showcasing books, departing from the conventional layout of
smaller rooms typically associated with older bookshops.
Instead, the store is grand and vast—like Brazil itself.

Upon entry through the pivoting doors, which serve as
both shelving units and a window display, visitors are
presented a small, low-ceilinged entrance hall displaying magazines. This intentional juxtaposition heightens
the transition into the expansive, high-ceilinged room
where books take center stage. Wooden shelving, rising
gracefully to a height of 2.5 meters (8 feet), curves
through the center of the hall, enveloping the pillars
without obscuring them.

The organic design of the shelves creates intimate nooks
and corners throughout the space, ideal for browsing
and reading—a defining characteristic of all Livraria da
Vila sites.

**Location:**
São Paulo, Brazil
**Year:**
2012
**Photography:**
Fernando Guerra

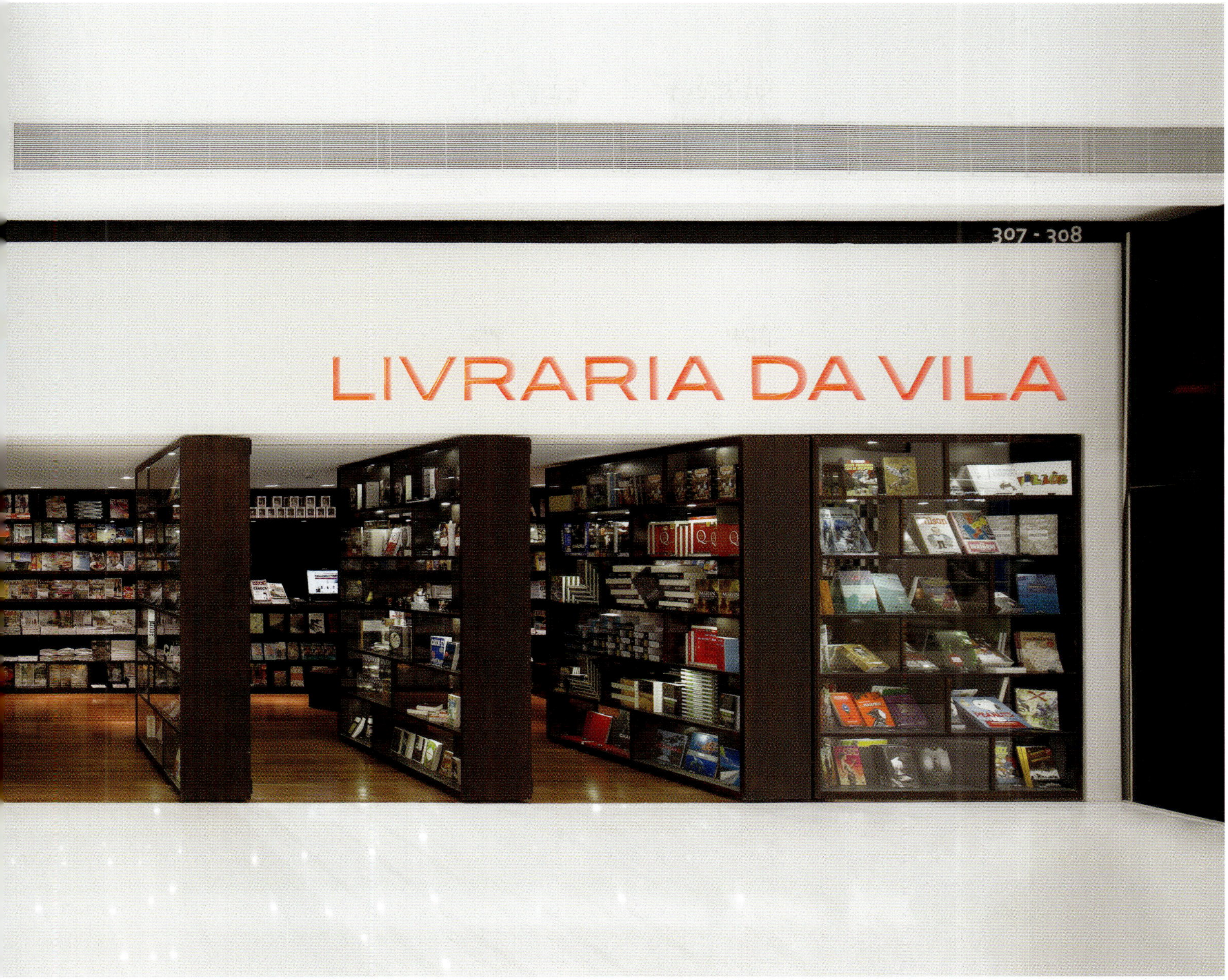
307 - 308
LIVRARIA DA VILA

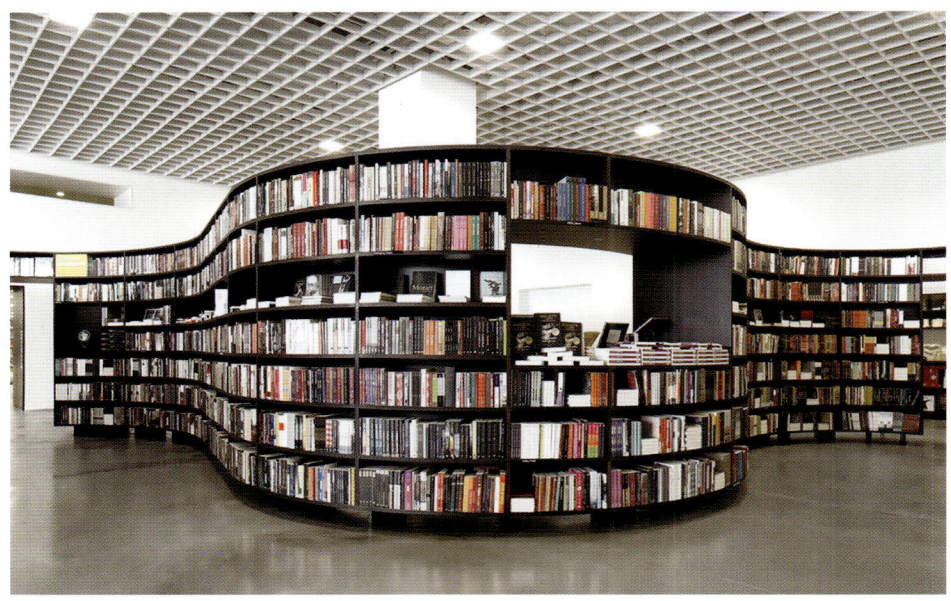

Literatura
Estrangeira

Arte
Culinária

# CLUBE CHOCOLATE

Clube Chocolate is a multi-brand concept store split into three floors, with a restaurant in the basement. It is in the hip Jardins neighborhood of São Paulo.

The long and narrow plot determined the layout of the building, dividing it into two sections along a longitudinal axis: On one side, a void spans across all floors, ensuring ample natural light in all spaces; on the other side, there are large openings for displaying products, along with restrooms, storage rooms, and administrative areas.

The very small size of the plot and the short construction time frame called for a mixed construction system, combining metal and reinforced concrete. At the top, large trussed metal beams rest on concrete volumes that support the lower floors with cables.

From the street, after passing through a long corridor with the storefront, shoppers come to a stainless steel walkway leading to the first level. A spiral staircase, entirely clad in brushed steel, both ascends to the upper floors and descends into the basement. A bar and restaurant open onto a garden of light-colored sand and palm trees, recalling Rio de Janeiro, where the Clube Chocolate brand was founded.

**Location:**
São Paulo, Brazil
**Year:**
2003
**Photography:**
Alvaro Povoa
Tuca Reinés

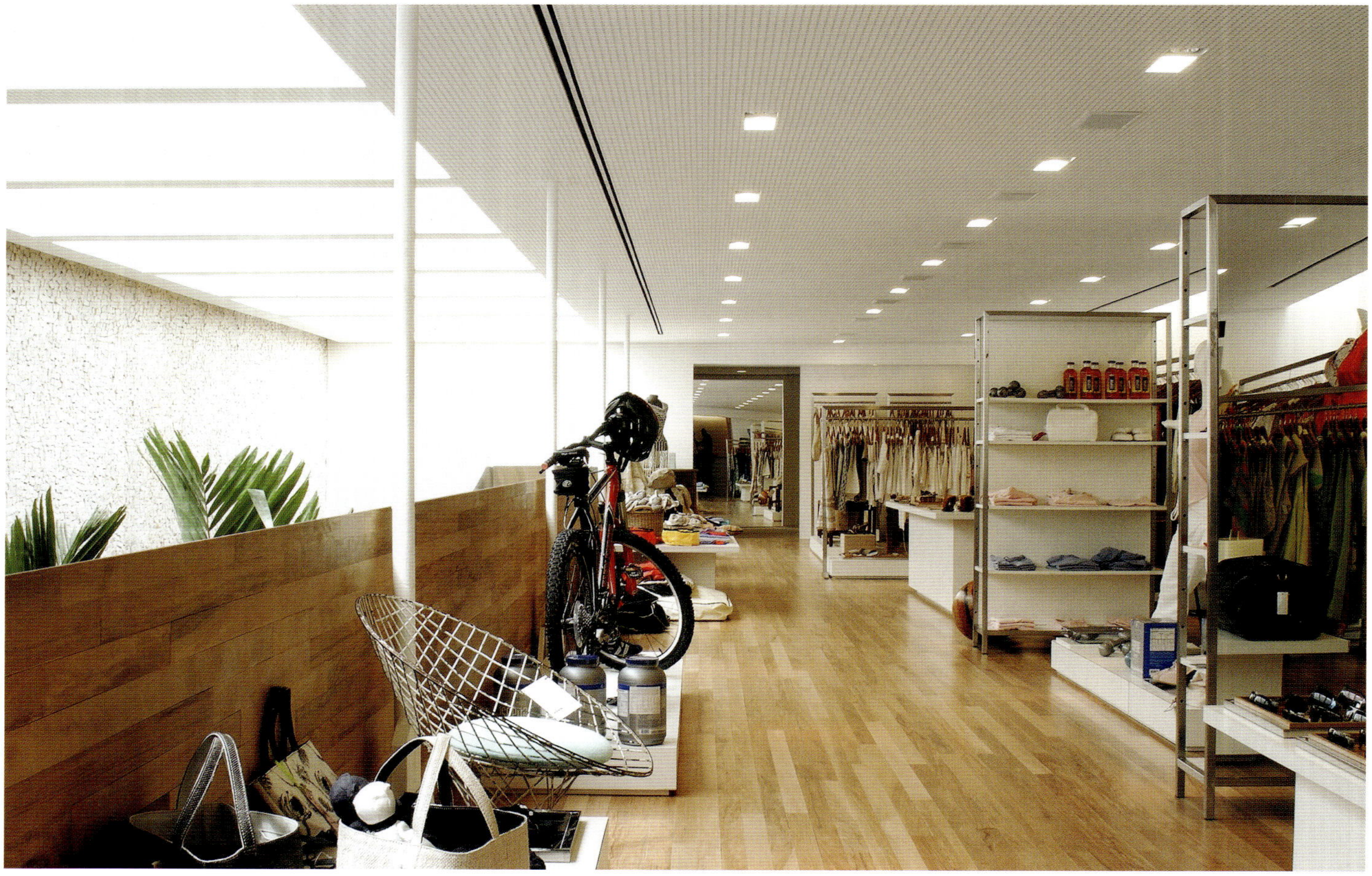

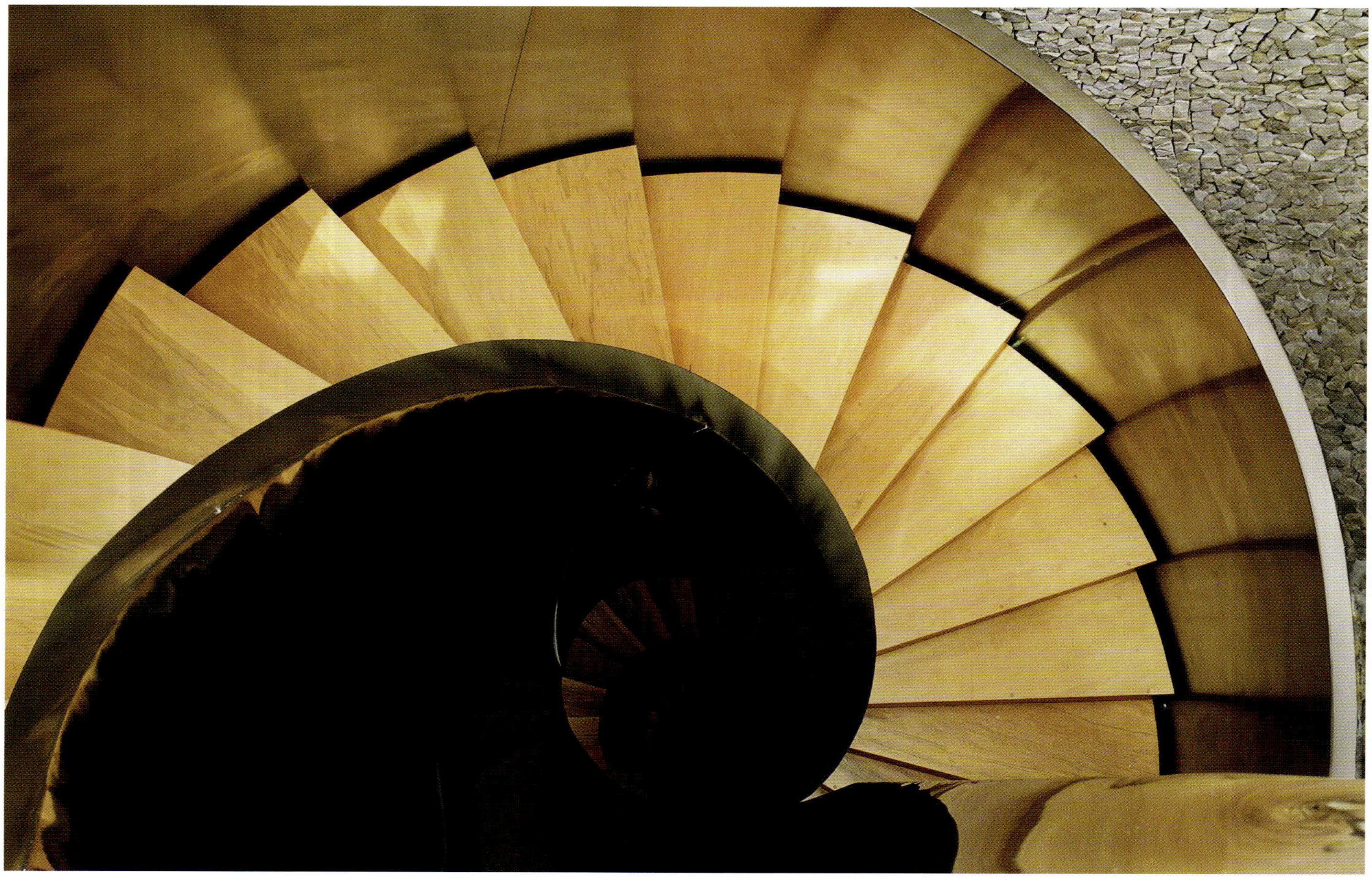

# DPOT

Dpot Mobiliário Brasileiro is a Brazilian furniture brand. This dpot occupies a 1,500 m² (16,150 ft.²) residential plot in São Paulo. Renovating and repurposing the structure to commercial use, the designers reorganized internal spaces and façades, while retaining the informal and relaxed ambience of the site's residential past. This transformation ensured that products could be displayed and arranged as if they were in a home. Varying ceiling heights and mezzanines introduced a scale unique to each room.

Two fundamental concepts in the store's design were to ensure that the garden remained visible from within the store and that the curated rooms be visible from the exterior. To achieve this, the lower section was opened up and an uninterrupted strip of glass installed around the entire perimeter, providing the desired transparency.

For the exterior cladding, cement panels were chosen for the upper section and wooden planks for the interiors. This integration between interior and exterior creates a sense of harmony, with seemingly floating volumes amid the lush garden surroundings.

**Location:**
São Paulo, Brazil
**Year:**
2015
**Photography:**
Fernando Guerra

# HAVAIANAS | RIO DE JANEIRO

Although now fashion icons, Havaianas sandals remain true to their humble roots: rubber flip-flops inspired by Japanese "zori" made from rice straw. Comfortable and stylish, since 1962 they've become essential for beachgoers and trendsetters alike.

This store in Rio de Janeiro marks Havaianas' expanded retail presence in Brazil. The goal was to capture the essence of the brand: freshness, informality, comfort, ease, well-being, and an *essência brasileira*.

The store emanates an informal vibe. It resembles an open square integrated into the sidewalk. Dispensing with traditional doors and window displays, the façade features lush greenery and abundant natural light. There is a metal grid alternating glass and wooden elements for ventilation and irrigation.

Unlike the São Paulo flagship store, this Rio de Janeiro location required a vertical layout spread across four floors due to the limited plot size. This called for the need to captivate customers throughout the space. Thus, the façade, resembling a black box, deviates from the expected Havaianas aesthetic, eliciting curiosity about its contents.

The ground floor, accessible from the street, seamlessly extends the sidewalk, devoid of doors or window displays. Lush vegetation complements the polished stainless-steel wall covering, acting as a mirror and maintaining an air of mystery about the upper floors. Operating as a square, customers are effortlessly drawn inside, where the store gradually reveals itself.

The upper floors, characterized by slabs of varying sizes and contours, feature translucent stairs revealing a colored gradient of Havaianas sandals—a nod to the brand's flagship product. Displayed on all four walls up to the top floor, the sandals are showcased under a white checkered glass pergola, allowing natural light to illuminate the space and accentuate the products.

**Location:**
Rio de Janeiro, Brazil
**Year:**
2018
**Photography:**
Fernando Guerra

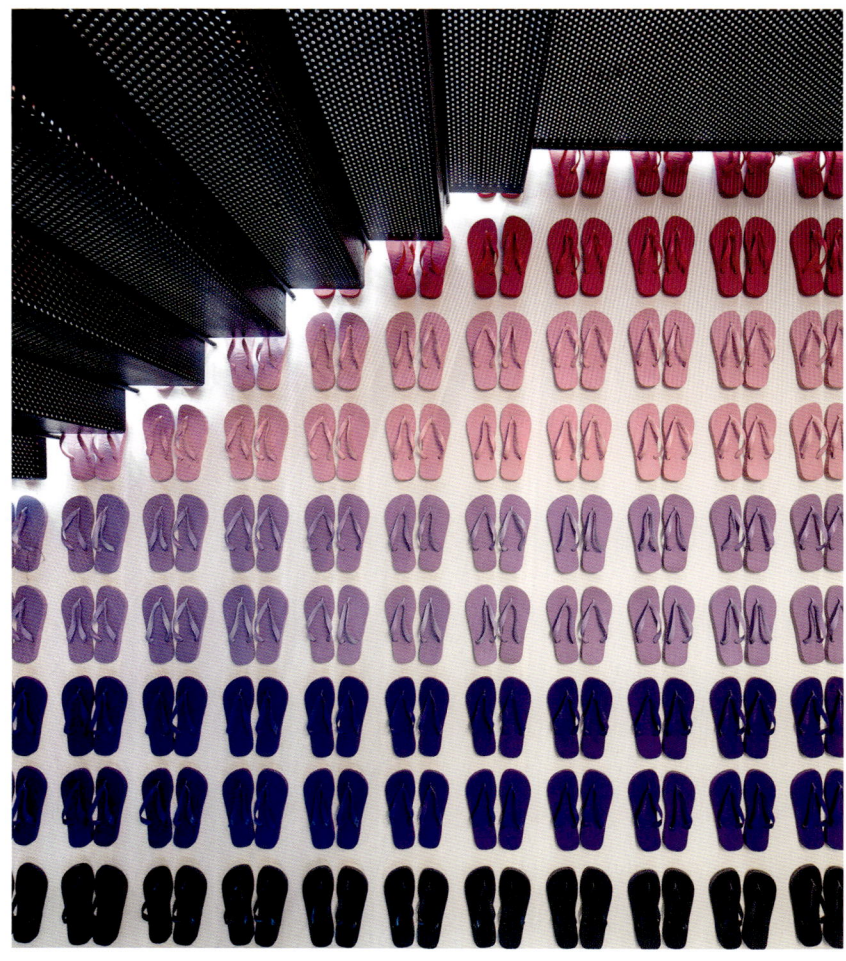

# PAULA RAIA

Brazilian fashion designer Paula Raia had a vision: a store with retail space and couture workroom under one roof. To achieve this, an existing São Paulo building underwent renovations and extensions to accommodate a complex program. The result is the designer's signature pale/nude color minimalism expressed architecturally.

The entrance hallway, with its soaring double-height ceiling, sets the tone with a wall adorned in layers of fabrics, embodying the essence of the garments sold. Natural light floods the space through a domed skylight and the façade glass, allowing a beautiful tree in the garden below to thrive. A rustic stone bench adds to the casual ambience.

Stepping into the store, visitors encounter merchandising areas, fitting rooms, and the cashier. Sinuous brass racks complement the space, offering views of the garden below. Above, a mezzanine houses the storage room and the evening gown design team. On the lower floor, prêt-a-porter designers, seamstresses for in-store alterations, pattern-cutting areas, and more coalesce. A newly built outbuilding accommodates the creation room, where designers work alongside fitting areas.

The façade underwent a complete redesign, with laminated glass panels incorporating fabrics, providing glimpses into the store without compromising privacy. The color palette, spanning walls, floors, carpets, drapes, and furnishings, echoes the hues found in the garments, creating a cohesive aesthetic throughout.

**Location:**
São Paulo, Brazil
**Year:**
2018
**Photography:**
Fernando Guerra

# INSTITUTO LING

The Instituto Ling, a Brazilian cultural foundation, is headquartered at a corner in the Três Figueiras neighborhood of Porto Alegre. The building is slightly raised from the ground and seems to be an object hovering amid a garden. The main façade, to the southeast, is practically solid—the one opening is the entry door, accessible through a winding ramp that rises above the garden. By contrast, the southwest façade is lighter and more transparent, with vertical fins to control the lighting from the interior.

From the entrance, visitors go along a succession of galleries. Each section along these galleries opens differently; they are devised to control incoming light. In the café there is an alternation between a solid wall and a glass pane extending from floor to ceiling, with doors opening onto an open-air terrace. Finally, there is the exhibition area and the auditorium vestibule, both flooded with abundant natural light.

Finishes along the circulation/gallery are neutral, with white walls and ceilings and gray concrete flooring. The supporting areas have wood-paneled walls.

To the right of the main entrance is access to classrooms, meeting rooms, restrooms, and the stairs to the lower level. This level houses the events hall, the show kitchen for classes, a tasting room, and an administrative area. The kitchen was designed to hold cooking classes, but also serves to accommodate events. It is connected to a tasting room—with a twelve-seat dining table—integrated with the side garden.

The prevailing finishes throughout are white walls and ceilings and hardwood flooring. Furthermore, the building features a second basement with parking, storage rooms, technical areas, and staff locker rooms.

**Location:**
São Paulo, Brazil
**Year:**
2011
**Photography:**
Leonardo Finotti

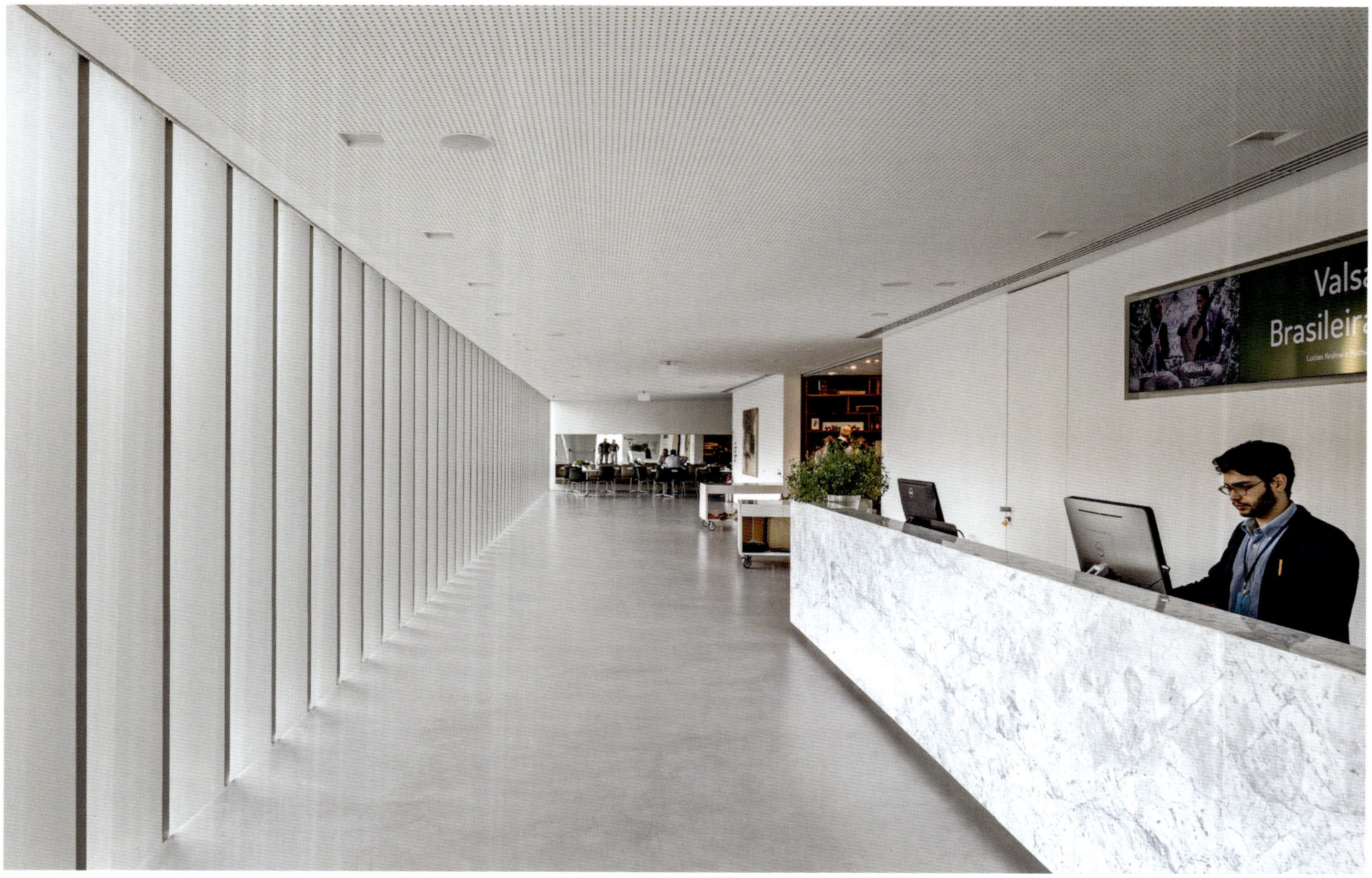
Valsa
Brasileira

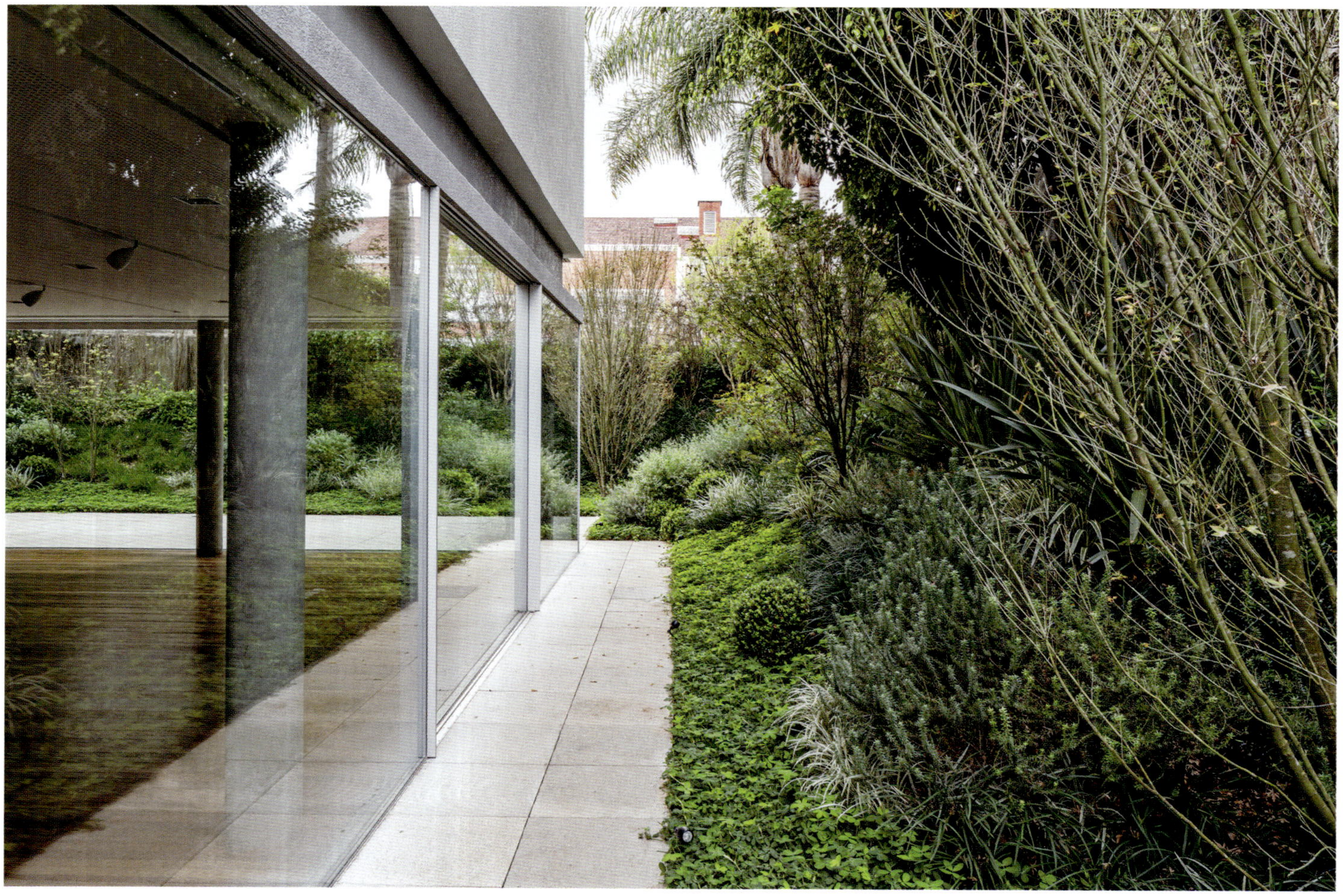

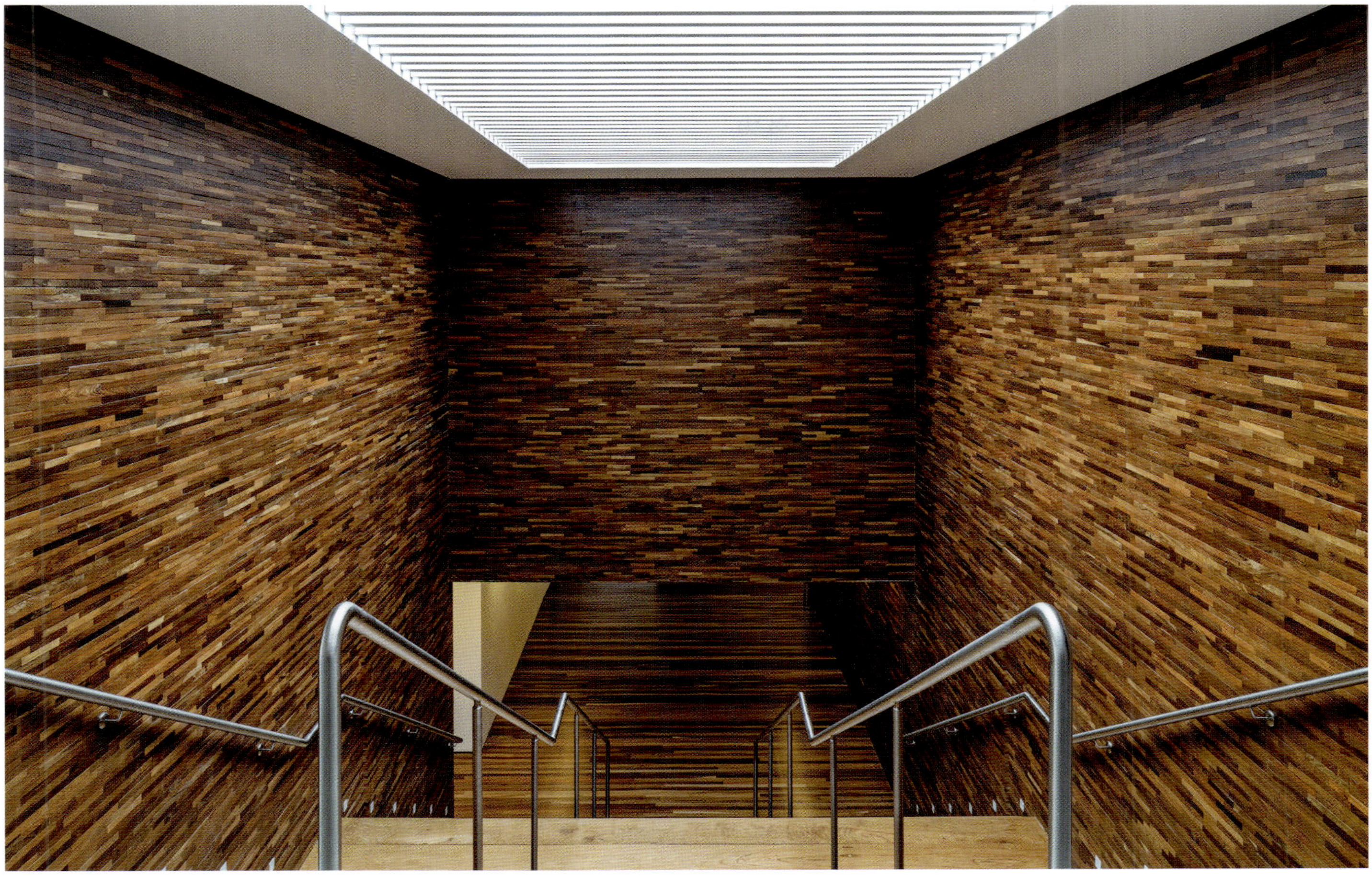

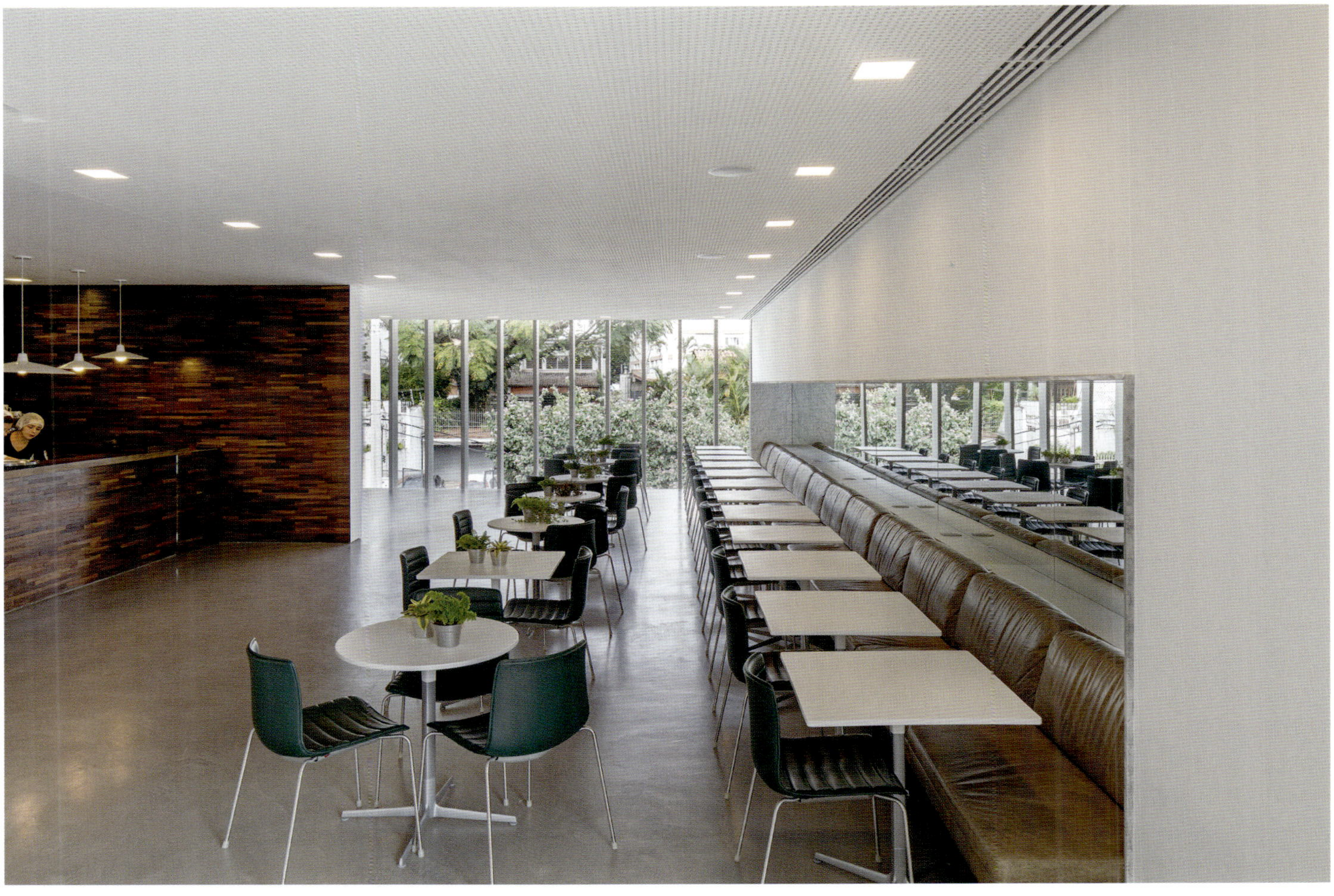

FOUR

# PRIVATE RESIDENCES

# CORAL HOUSE

The Coral House site was generated by the union of two smaller lots, the site now totaling 2,944.5 m² (31,692.5 ft.²). The sprawling home covers 2,750.7 m² (29,604.59 ft.²) and was designed for a couple with three children. The program included a spacious social area to accommodate large family gatherings.

The owner breeds fish for a hobby. Thus, the program included a large indoor aquarium and reflecting pool at the entrance patio. Designing the 4.8 m³ (169 ft.³) saltwater aquarium was a challenge that ultimately became a partition between the home theater and the study. A large area was set aside in the basement for the complex saltwater treatment.

The placement of the house provides a back garden. To correct an irregularity in the plot, an area at the rear of the garden was enclosed to accommodate gym and massage rooms, a playroom, locker rooms, and a small kitchen. A 25-meter (82-foot) swimming pool is adjacent to this smaller building and rounds out the leisure area.

The ground floor houses the entire social area and part of the service area. The upper level contains the private quarters and access to the rooftop. Parking and the remainder of the service areas are located in the basement level, dotted with several small patios to ensure ventilation and natural lighting.

The street façade is inconspicuous, with no apparent windows, aiming to preserve privacy as much as possible. Due to the recurring floods in the region, the ground floor of the house was raised 1 meter (3 feet) above street level.

**Location:**
São Paulo, Brazil
**Year:**
2020
**Photography:**
Manuel Sá

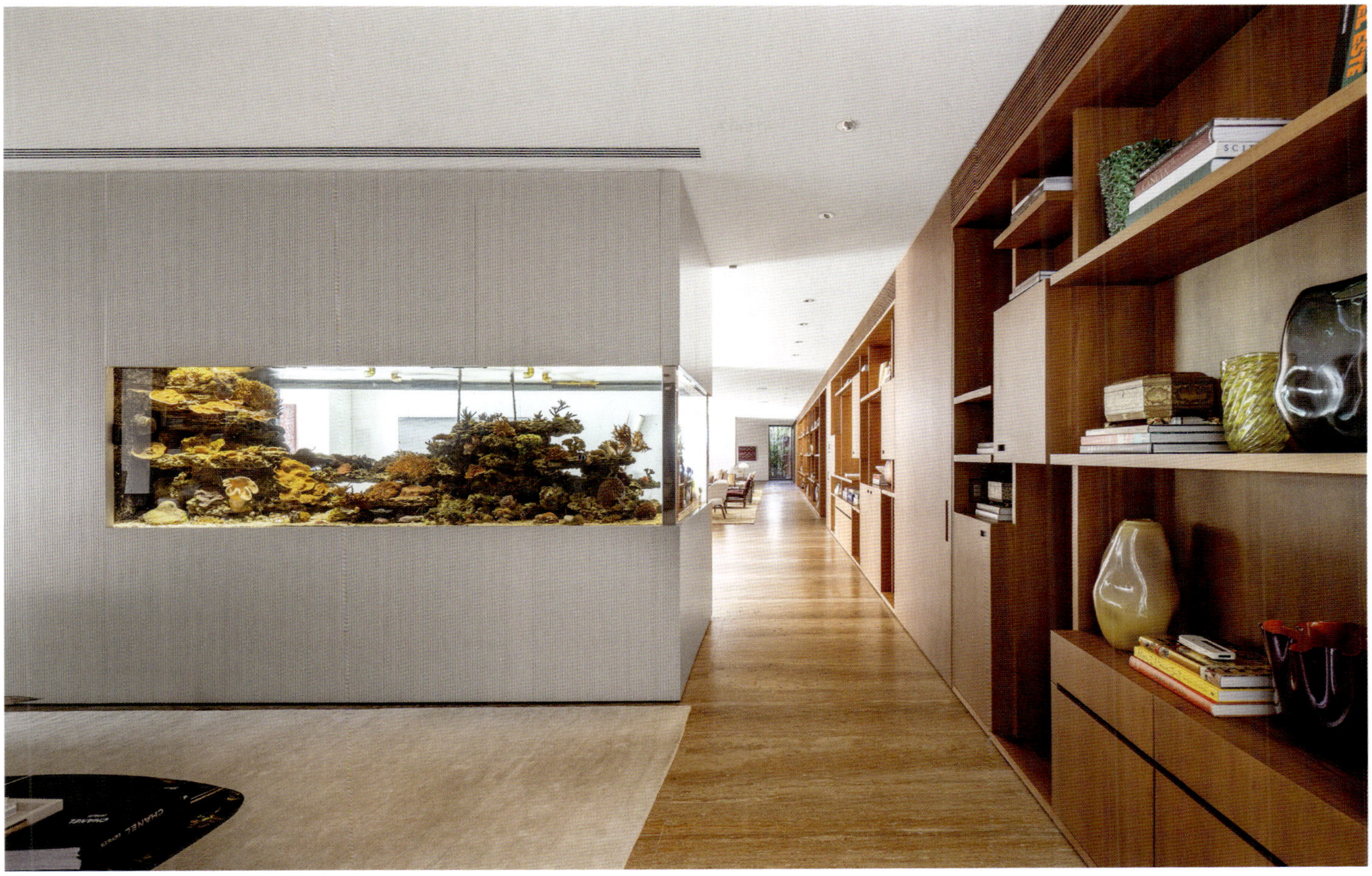

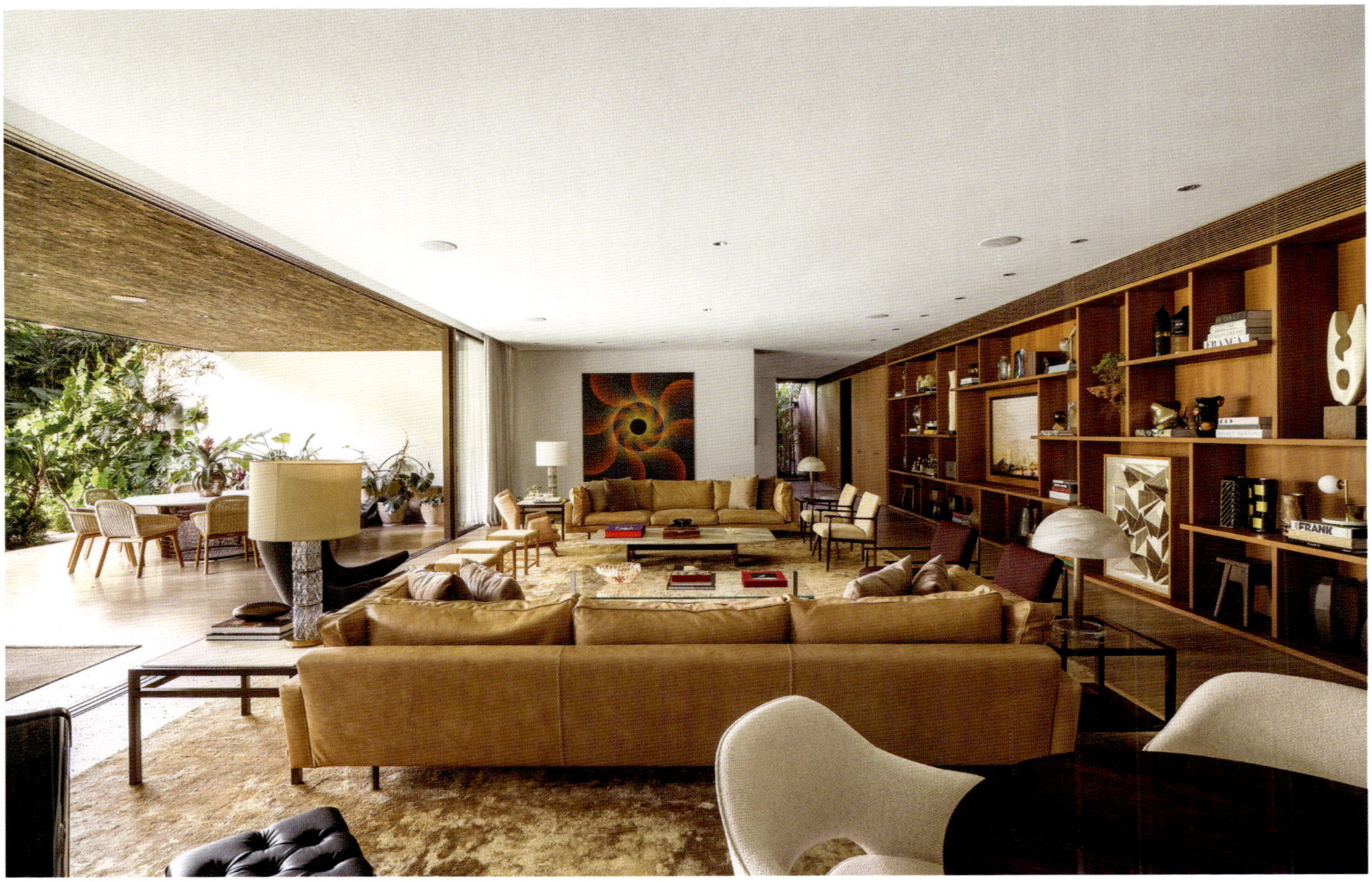

# LA HOUSE

Designed for an active family and located in Los Angeles's tony Bel Air neighborhood, this house exudes a tranquil confidence.

It is arrayed on three levels: The upper level is conceived as a private refuge for bedrooms and a family room. The intermediate room is the most "public" in the house and contains formal living and dining areas where the couple entertain guests. The semi-subterranean first floor accommodates a garage, staff quarters, mechanical rooms, wine cellar, game room, and terrace, all of which open onto a small garden that extends to the swimming pool deck.

The exterior of lime wash is composed of simple, orthogonal forms like precise window openings, perpendicular walls, and a seamless glass railing that is barely visible. Cantilevers give the structure the appearance of floating above the surrounding Mediterranean flora. As if a deliberate break from the precise white geometry, an entrance door by Brazilian artist Hugo França is raw tropical wood, brown and gnarled, smooth and warm to the touch.

LA House is the purposeful inverse of the effusive mansions one usually finds in Bel Air and nearby Beverly Hills. It is a modern, family-oriented, and intensely private intervention into the Southern California landscape.

**Location:**
Los Angeles, United States
**Year:**
2020
**Photography:**
Fernando Guerra

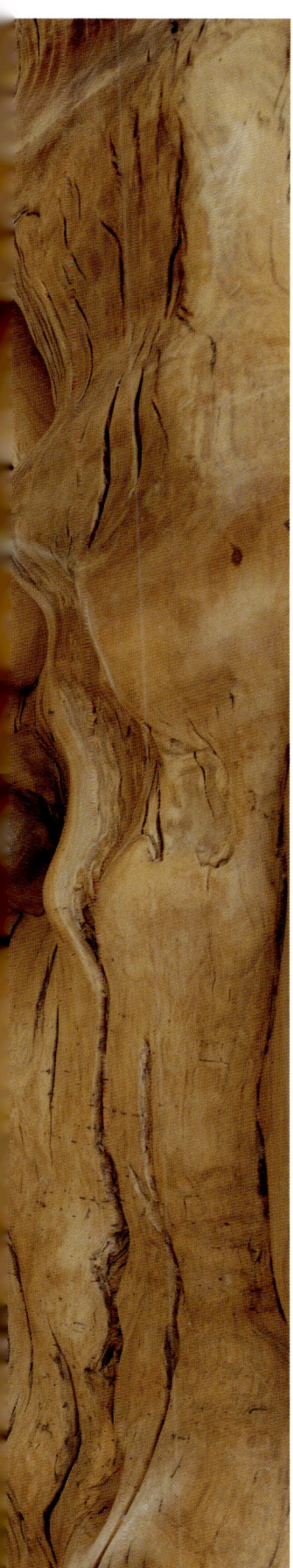

# FAZENDA TRÊS PEDRAS

The project for Fazenda Três Pedras ("Three Stones Farm") presented a unique challenge involving the restoration of 19th-century farm buildings of historical significance. The Três Pedras estate is located in Campinas in the state of São Paulo.

Situated on a sprawling 25-hectare (61.7-acre) property, the main house, constructed in 1871, along with ancillary structures like the caretaker's lodging, living quarters for enslaved persons, and storage facilities, all required adaptation to modern uses while adhering to stringent heritage protection laws. Despite undergoing previous renovations, the house lacked essential amenities, rendering it unsuitable for the client's intended purposes as a place to gather family and friends over the weekend or, eventually, to live after retirement.

The primary challenge lay in modernizing the space with minimal interventions, ensuring that any new additions were distinctly separate from the original architecture. To achieve this, boxlike containers were introduced to fulfill modern requirements, such as bathrooms and closets clad in copper, and stairs encased in leather. These containers were constructed independently of the existing structure, positioned lower than the ceiling of the house, to maintain a clear distinction between original and added elements.

There is a chapel on the property that was renovated to preserve its original character. The caretakers' lodge was repurposed into a fitness room, the former slave quarters into guest rooms, and the old storage facility into a small chapel, each equipped with modern amenities. Adjacent to the woods, a leisure pavilion and swimming pool were constructed. These structures were designed to be simple and discreet, ensuring they complement rather than compete with the splendid colonial architecture of the existing buildings.

**Location:**
Campinas, Brazil
**Year:**
2005
**Photography:**
Cristiano Mascaro
Leonardo Finotti

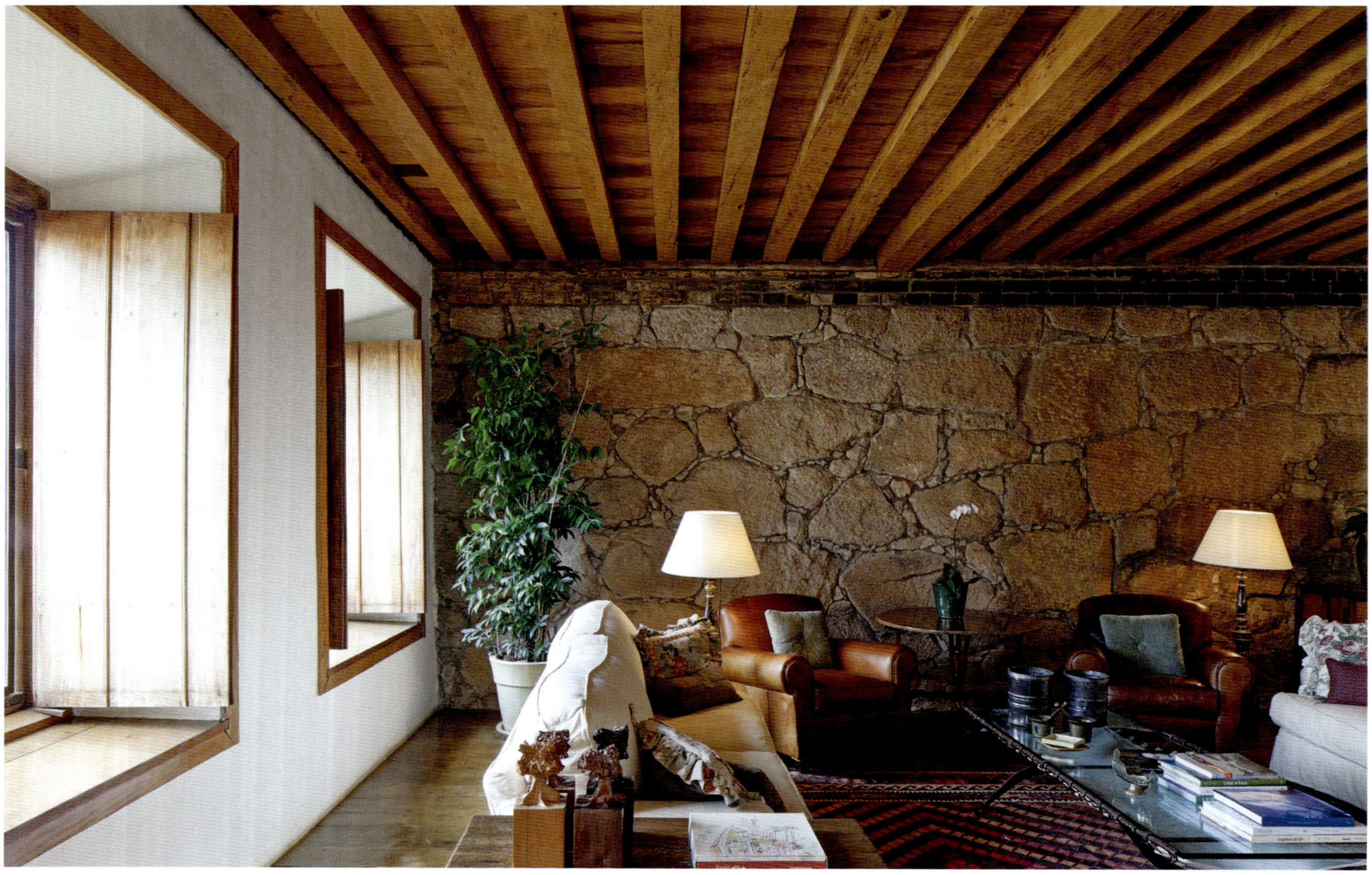

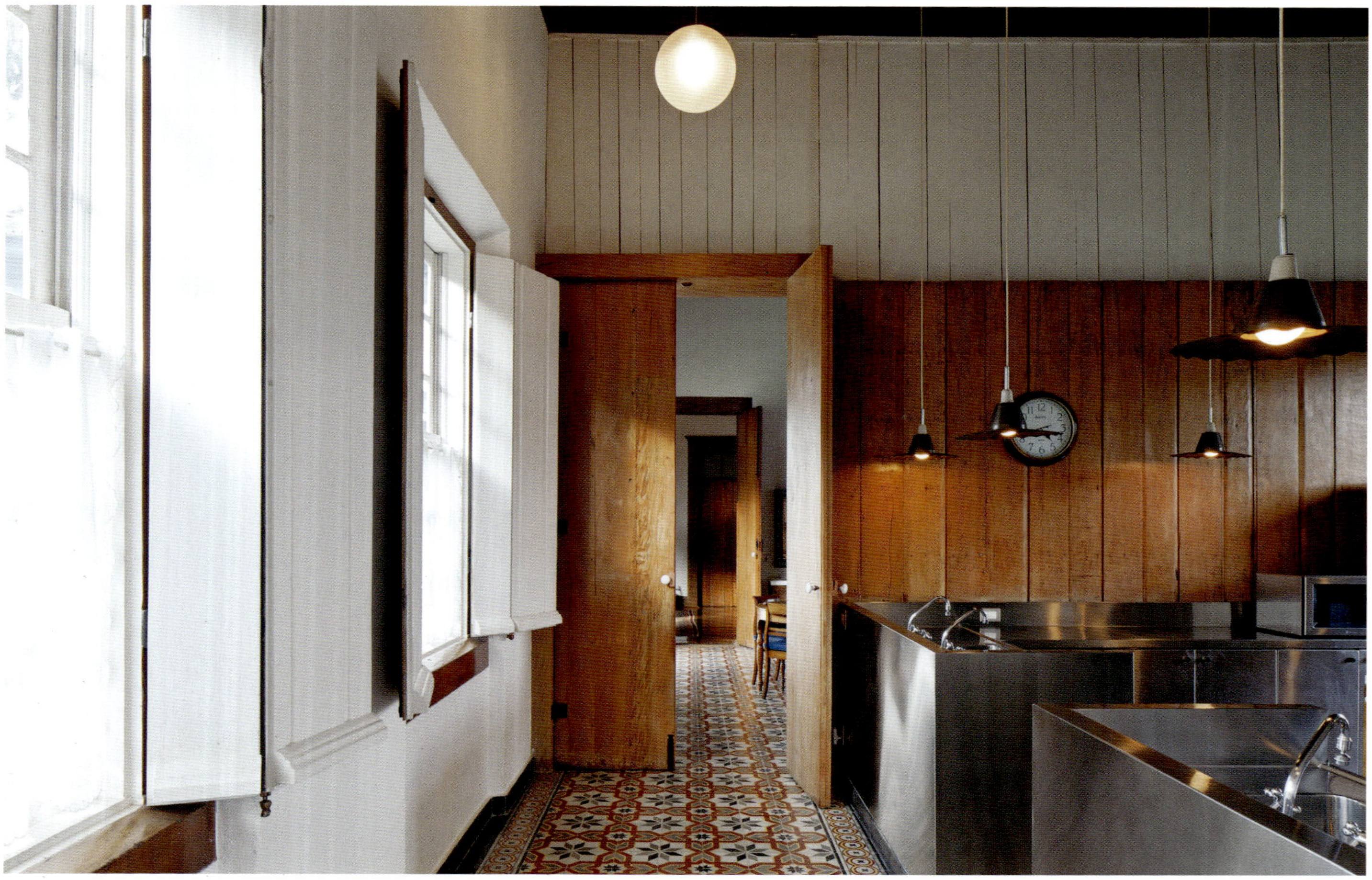

# IPORANGA HOUSE

Along the coast of Iporanga, in the Atlantic Forest region, southeast of São Paulo, the Iporanga House is designed to accommodate a family of Middle Eastern heritage. Located in Guarujá, 150 kilometers (93 miles) from the center of São Paulo, the house is a getaway home for the family. The property includes coconut trees, bromeliads, and other plants native to the region.

The property's boundaries and expansive beachfront are delineated from neighboring lots. The architectural composition comprises two sleek white volumes, one atop the other. The lower volume houses all social and service areas, seamlessly integrating living and dining spaces that extend onto a veranda. There are panoramic views of the swimming pool and the Atlantic Ocean beyond.

The upper volume has a striking feature: a mashrabiya screen, a nod to the owners' Middle Eastern roots, is meticulously crafted from aluminum and painted white, enveloping all five bedrooms, including the master suite, the latter commanding ocean views. Adjacent to the swimming pool, a tranquil sunken sitting area provides a setting for alfresco dining or relaxation.

**Location:**
Guarujá, Brazil
**Year:**
2006
**Photography:**
Leonardo Finotti
Nelson Kon

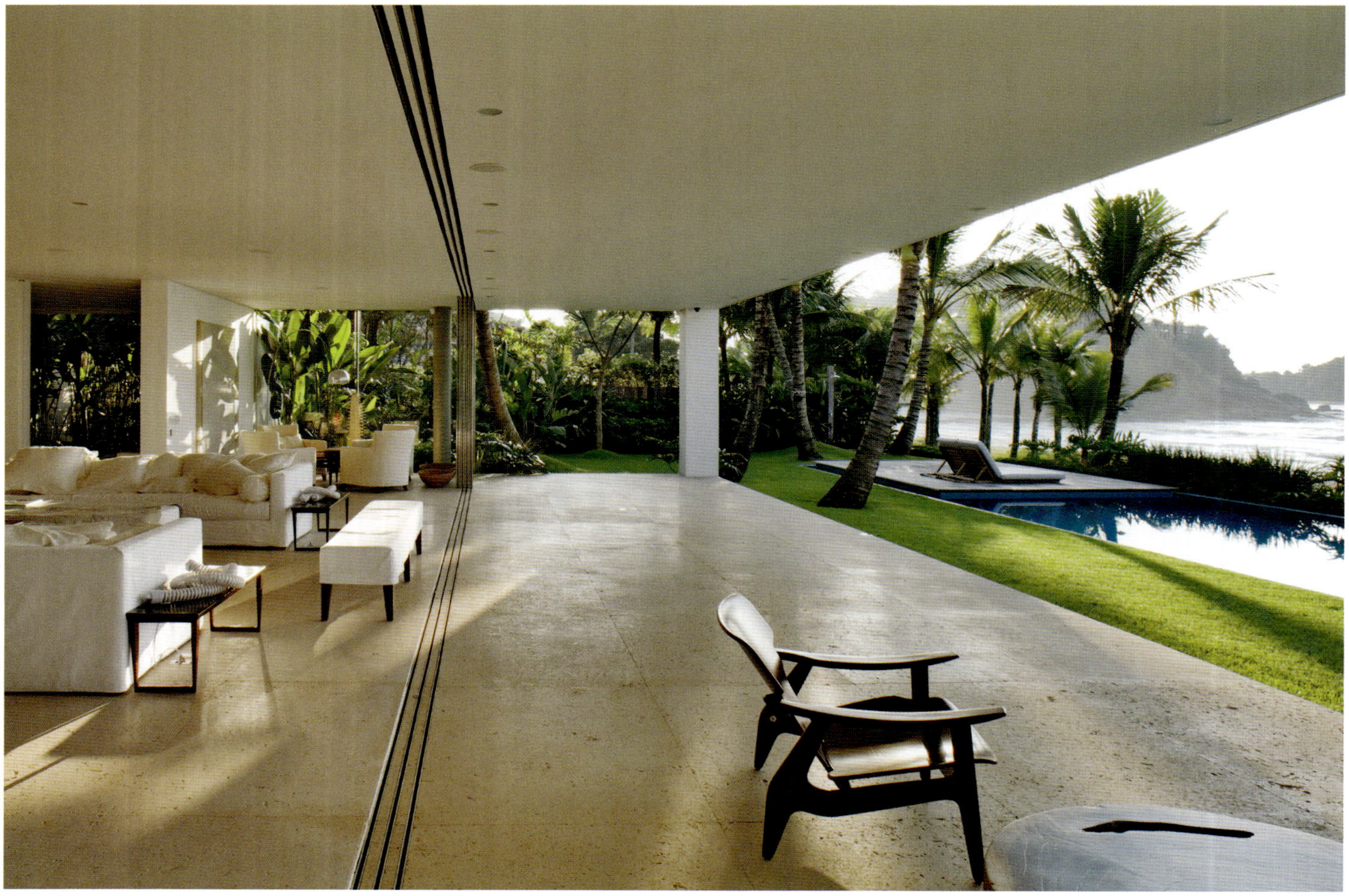

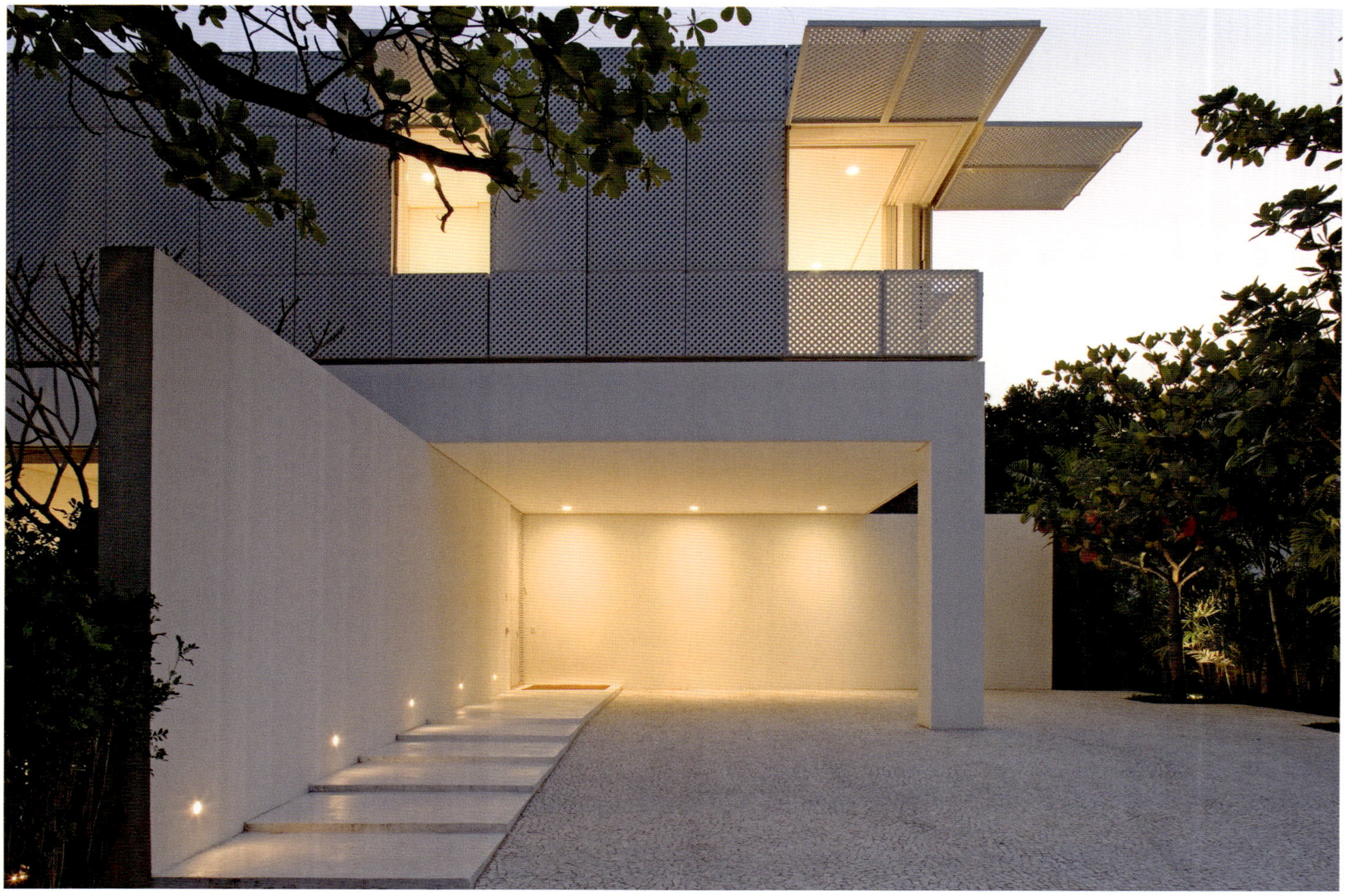

IPORANGA HOUSE

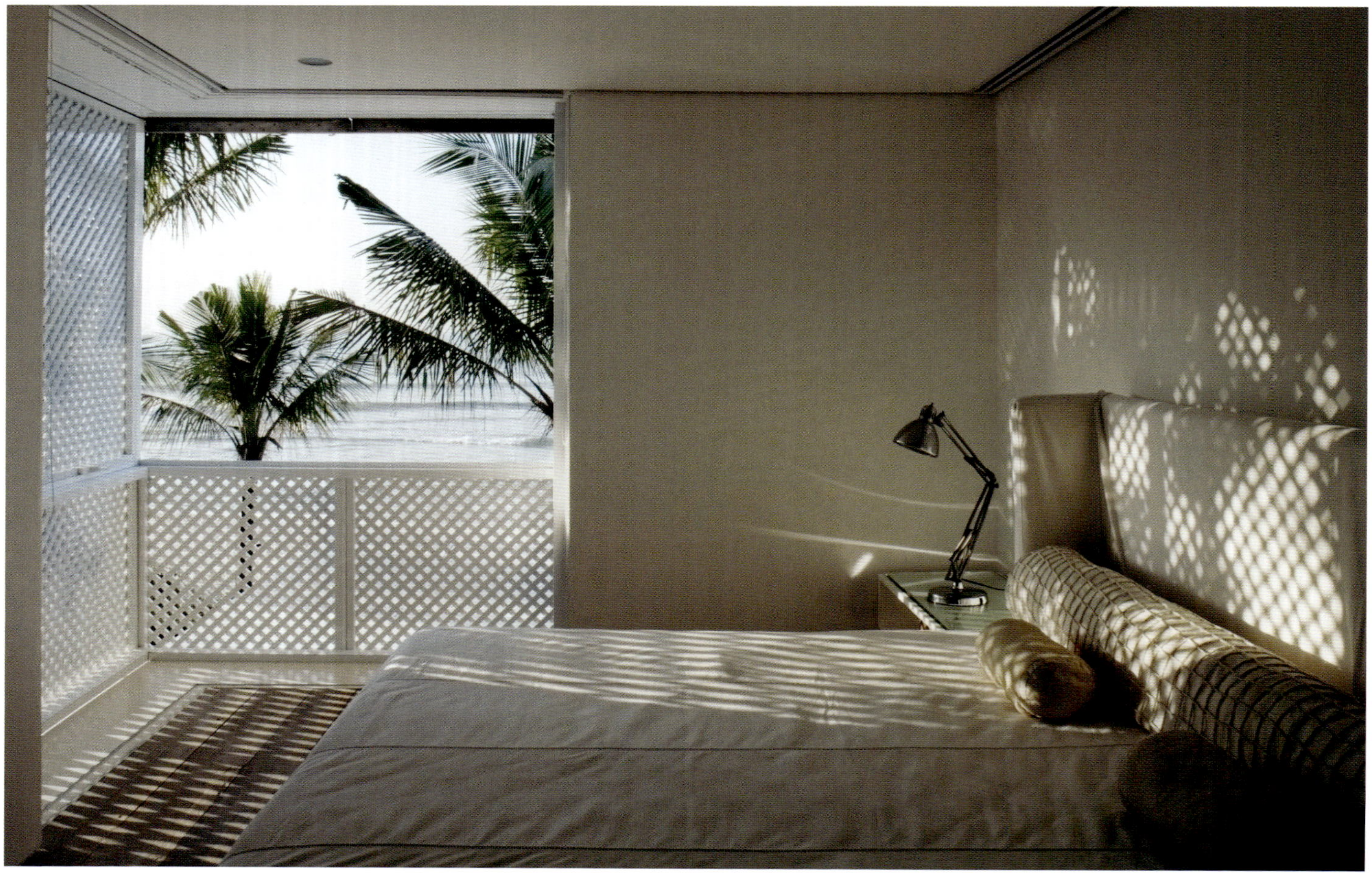

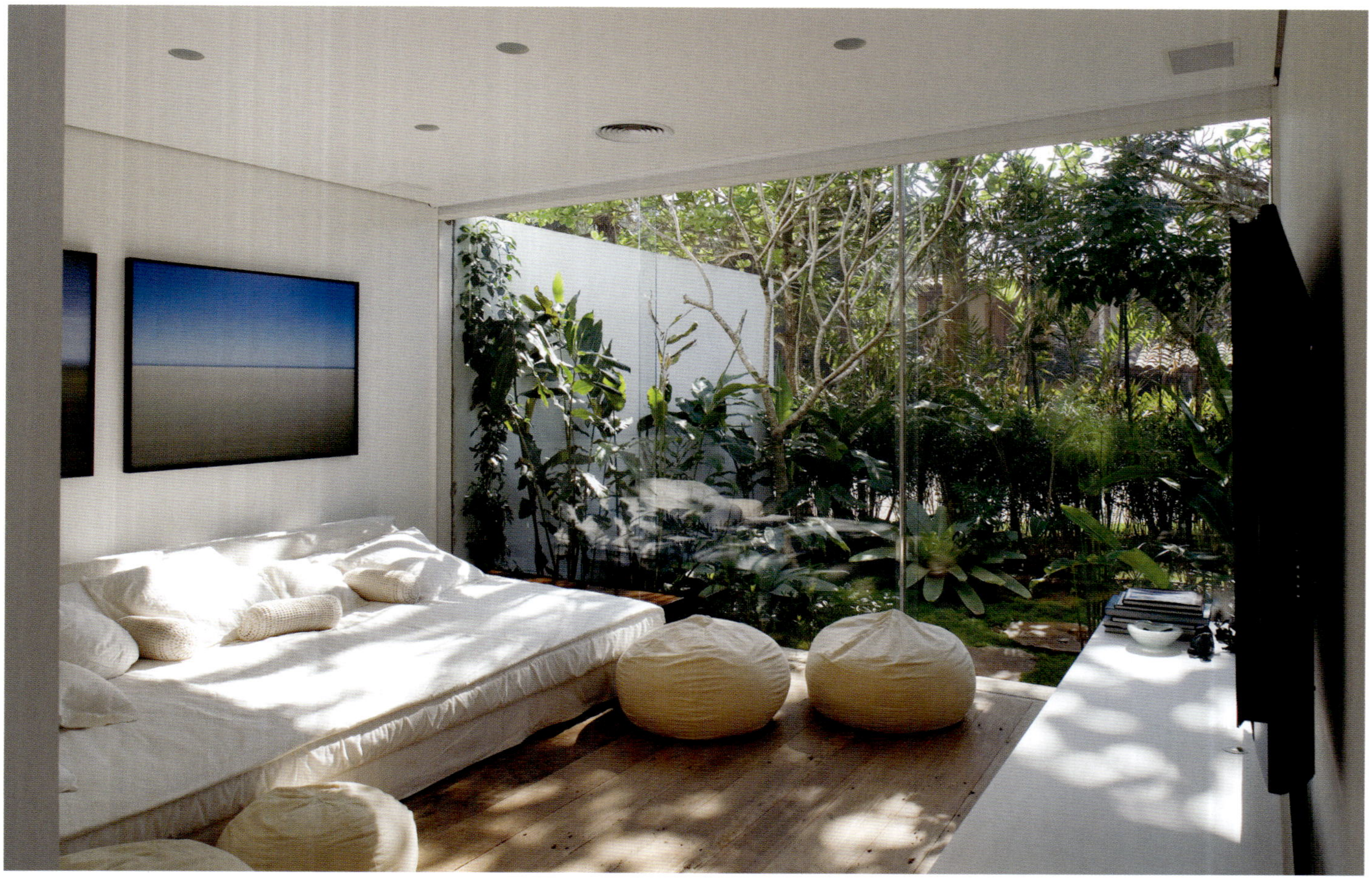

# 65 APARTMENT

This apartment in a pre-war building in Manhattan has been completely remodeled to accommodate four bedrooms, a study, a spacious living room, a dining room, and all necessary supporting spaces.

Wood paneling defines all shared rooms in the apartment and makes the space an urban refuge for the clients. Upon entering, one spies the foyer clad entirely in wood—walls and floors alike—and furnished with two benches and a pair of wall lamps by Jean Royère, a French interior designer whose work spans the 1930s through the 1960s.

The hallway ahead leads to the dining room at one end, featuring a crystal chandelier hanging over an antique table and chairs by Sérgio Rodrigues, a mid-century Brazilian designer. At the opposite end, the hallway leads to a living room with two distinct seating areas— one more informal, for watching TV and spending time with family; the other a more "shared" atmosphere for entertaining guests.

The hallway walls are covered with white-painted wood panels, concealing a built-in bar and the doors to the children's and guest bedrooms, as well as the study. The master bedroom and nursery are accessed from the living room.

**Location:**
New York, United States
**Year:**
2008
**Photography:**
Leonardo Finotti

# PIRACICABA HOUSE

This house, in Piracicaba (250 kilometers [155 miles] from São Paulo), serves as a gathering venue for a family dispersed throughout the state of São Paulo. The 2,000 m² (21,500 ft.²) plot resulted from the combination of two corner lots in a gated community.

The placement of the house considered the contour of the land, and the house faces north to maximize sunlight exposure on bedrooms and social areas. The layout, across three floors and arranged in perpendicular axes, integrates with the natural contours of the land, providing access to the garden from any level.

The lower ground level, semisubterranean and positioned at the land's lowest point, accommodates storage areas, the mechanical room, and the garage, supported by grid pillars. The L-shaped ground floor, accessible from the street via a sinuous ramp, houses service areas and the living and dining room.

The spacious room, entirely encased in glass, overlooks the rear of the property and connects to the pool deck through large sliding doors. On the opposite side, it is shielded from the sun and street view by a long sun baffle made of vertical slabs placed irregularly along the façade.

The upper floor extends perpendicularly to the contour of the land, cantilevering toward the street on one end and resting on the higher section of the land on the other. It contains the bedrooms and a TV room, with the latter opening onto a large wooden deck built on the ceiling slab over the living and dining room.

The swimming pool is nestled within the L-shaped space formed by the social and service areas and the slope rising toward higher sections of the land.

**Location:**
Piracicaba, Brazil
**Year:**
2009
**Photography:**
Leonardo Finotti
Nelson Kon

# GRECIA HOUSE

Located in a residential area of São Paulo, Grecia House occupies a sprawling corner lot spanning 4,830 m² (51,990 ft.²). The house is vaguely mysterious, yielding its secrets only reluctantly.

Visitors approach the main entrance by traversing a scenic path through a wooded area and across a spacious front garden. As the house emerges, its distinct architectural composition becomes apparent. It is comprised of four interconnected blocks, each with a unique finish: pebble-blasted concrete panels for the living quarters, exposed concrete for the study, wood planks for the entertainment area, and sand-blasted concrete panels for the dining and service spaces.

For those arriving by car, a driveway located at the rear provides convenient access. Beyond the garage—which houses the owner's prized collection of antique cars—an indoor garden pathway leads to the main floor and a blend of living and entertainment spaces. A gym and recreation rooms are on the lower level and a sauna in the basement.

The siting of the house was influenced by existing trees. Small patios and gardens were meticulously integrated around these natural elements, ensuring ample natural light, optimal ventilation, and a serene (if mysterious) ambience.

**Location:**
São Paulo, Brazil
**Year:**
2009
**Photography:**
Leonardo Finotti
Fernando Guerra

# YUCATAN HOUSE

Situated in the Jardim América neighborhood of São Paulo, Yucatan House was designed for a young couple and their three children. As avid collectors of contemporary art, the couple envisioned a home that exuded a spacious, luminous, and relaxed atmosphere, fostering a close connection with nature while providing an ideal backdrop for showcasing their art collection.

The residence is composed of seven distinct boxlike volumes, each varying in size and finish, strategically positioned at the front of the property, allowing for a sprawling garden oasis at the rear. Upon entering, a striking feature—a long, flat surface adorned with black-painted aluminum plaques—guides visitors across the blocks, leading from the garage to the kitchen and finally to the dining room.

Adjacent to these primary volumes are four additional blocks, thoughtfully arranged to accommodate the daughter's and guest bedrooms, the sons' bedrooms, the master suite, and the TV room and gym. This deliberate layout creates expansive spaces among the volumes. Both the main living and family rooms are adorned with works from the couple's collection.

The centerpiece of the outdoor space is a pool that extends from the dining room to the rear of the property. The pool features a sophisticated combination of aquatic plants, fish, gravel, and other natural materials to filter and purify water, providing a more eco-friendly and chemical-free alternative to traditional swimming pools.

**Location:**
São Paulo, Brazil
**Year:**
2009
**Photography:**
Fernando Guerra

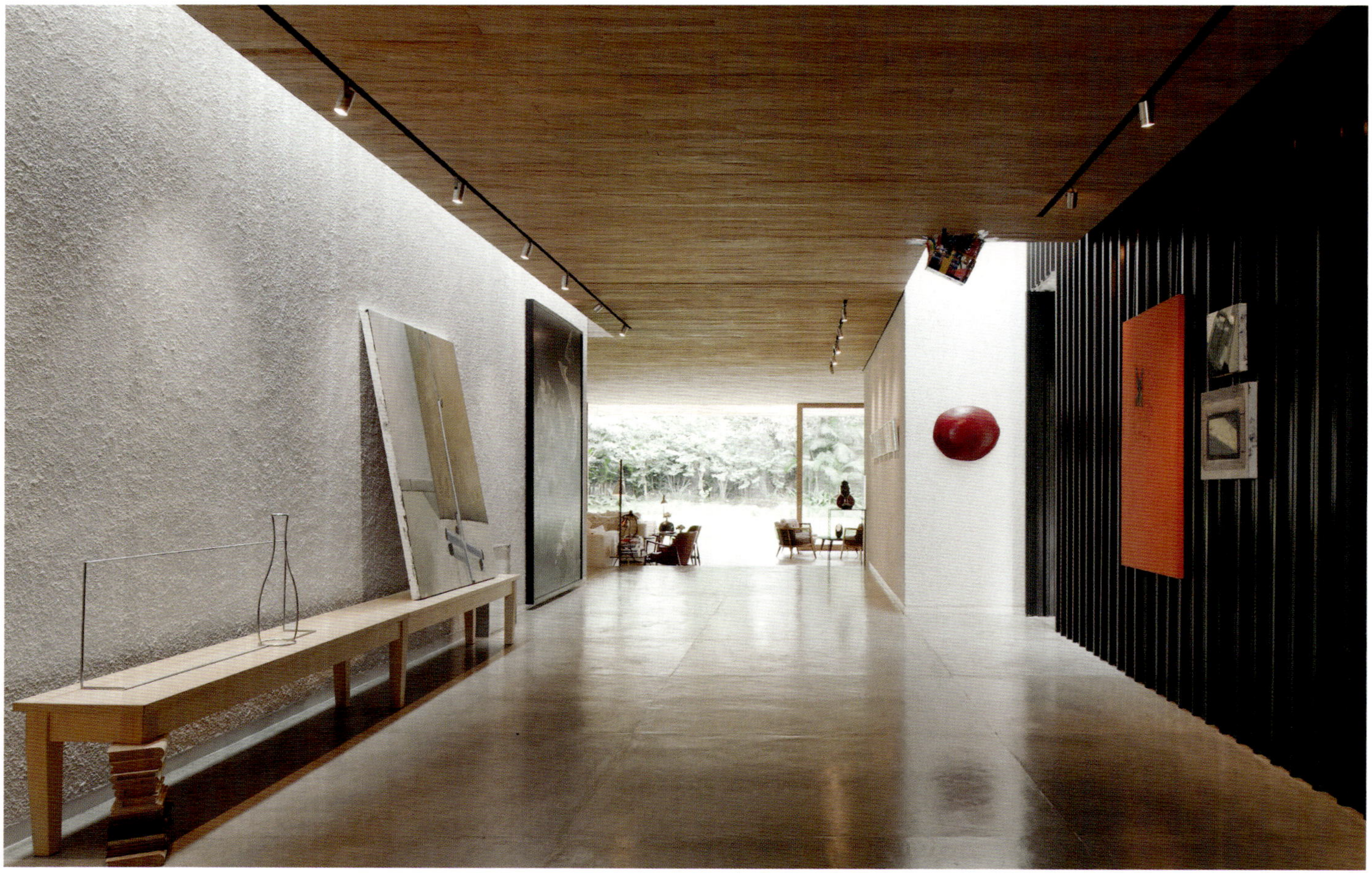

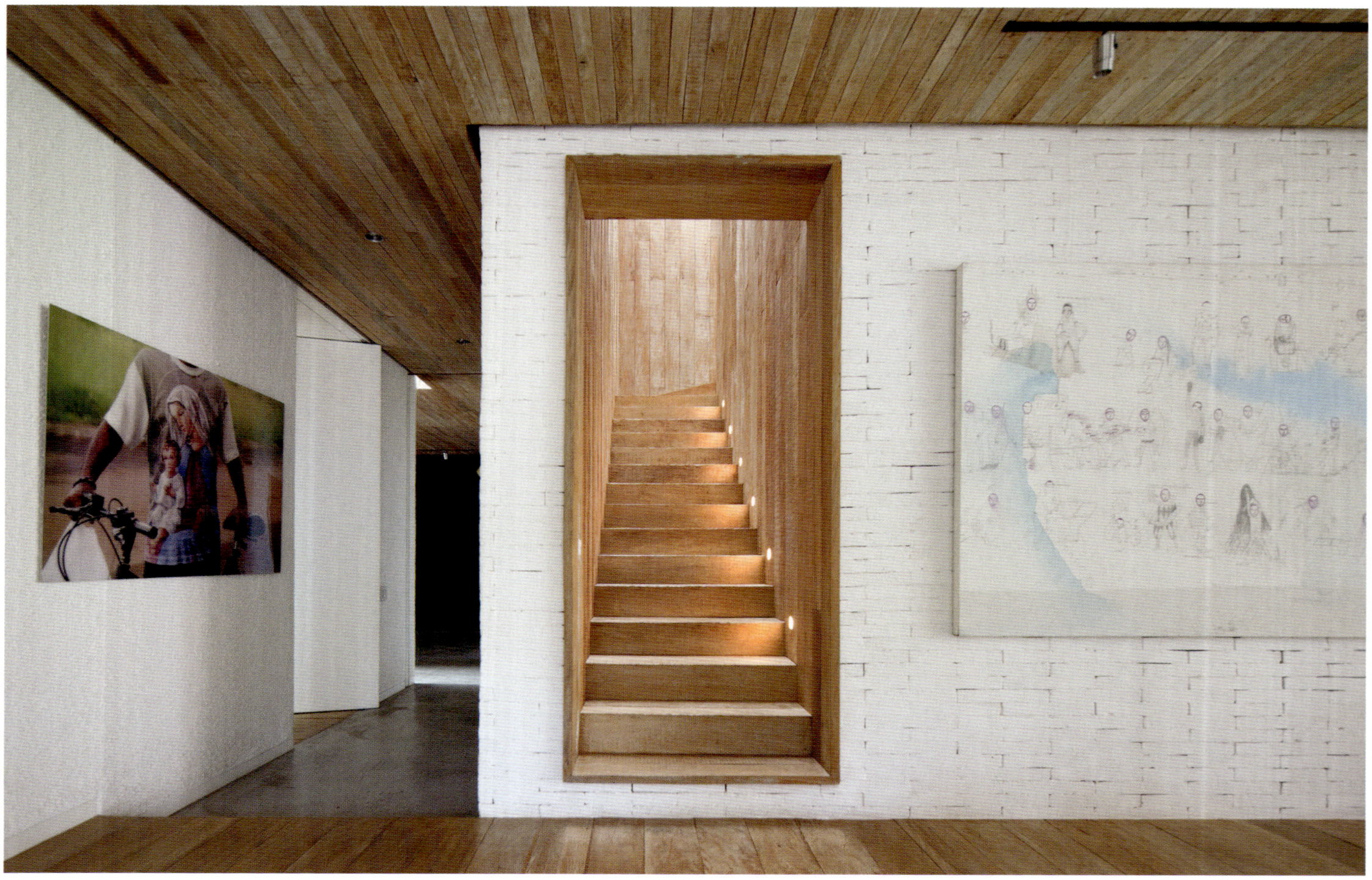

# CUBO HOUSE

Cubo House in São Paulo was created from a vision of an art-collecting couple and is a testament to their love of the arts. Conceived as a residence and a space for artists, the house is a striking cubic structure vertically divided into three levels and a mezzanine.

The entrance hall sets the stage for the main attraction: an expansive room with soaring double-height ceilings and a sleek polished concrete floor. This space serves multiple purposes—it hosts family gatherings and exhibitions and leads to a well-appointed kitchen and dining room.

The mezzanine is perched atop the service core. In the library, design takes center stage as a sprawling shelving unit adorns the back wall, complemented by a strip of fixed glass near the floor. A sculptural spiral staircase, clad in warm wood, entices guests to explore. It also leads to the private quarters upstairs—three bedrooms and a cozy private seating area.

Completing the assemblage, the basement houses essential spaces such as the garage and service areas. Cubo House combines form with function and is a haven for art and family life.

**Location:**
São Paulo, Brazil
**Year:**
2011
**Photography:**
Fernando Guerra

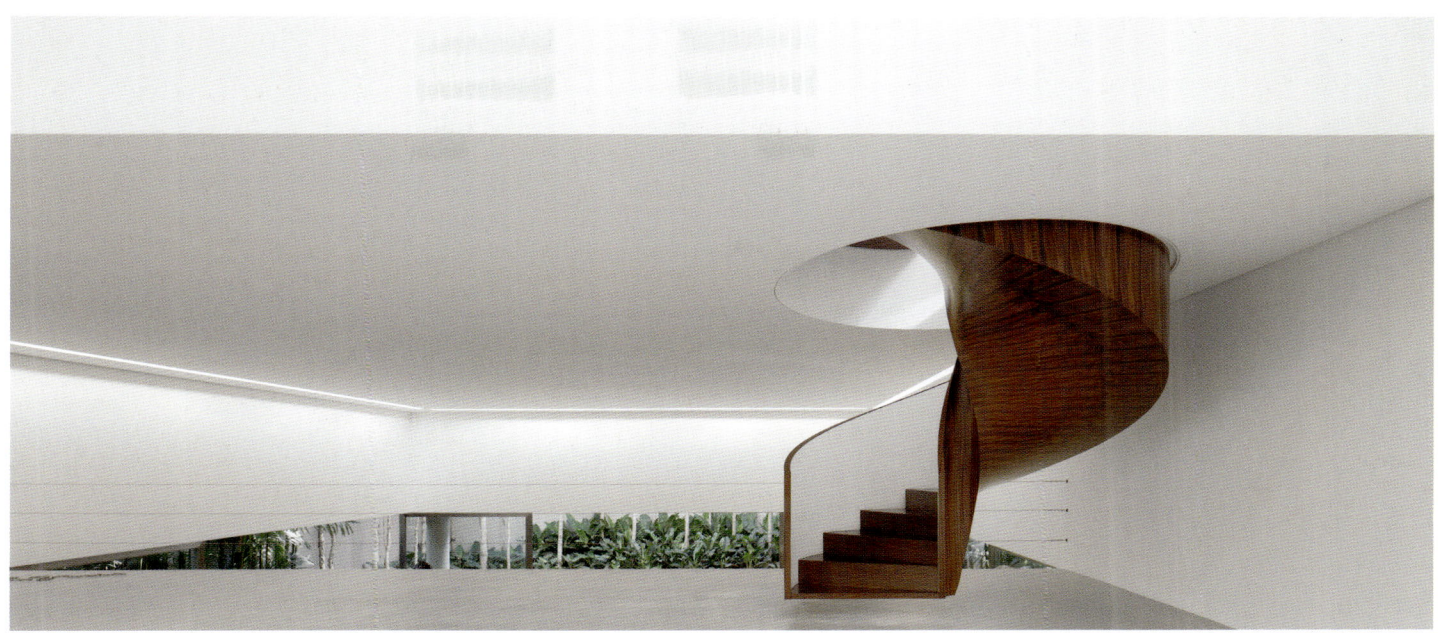

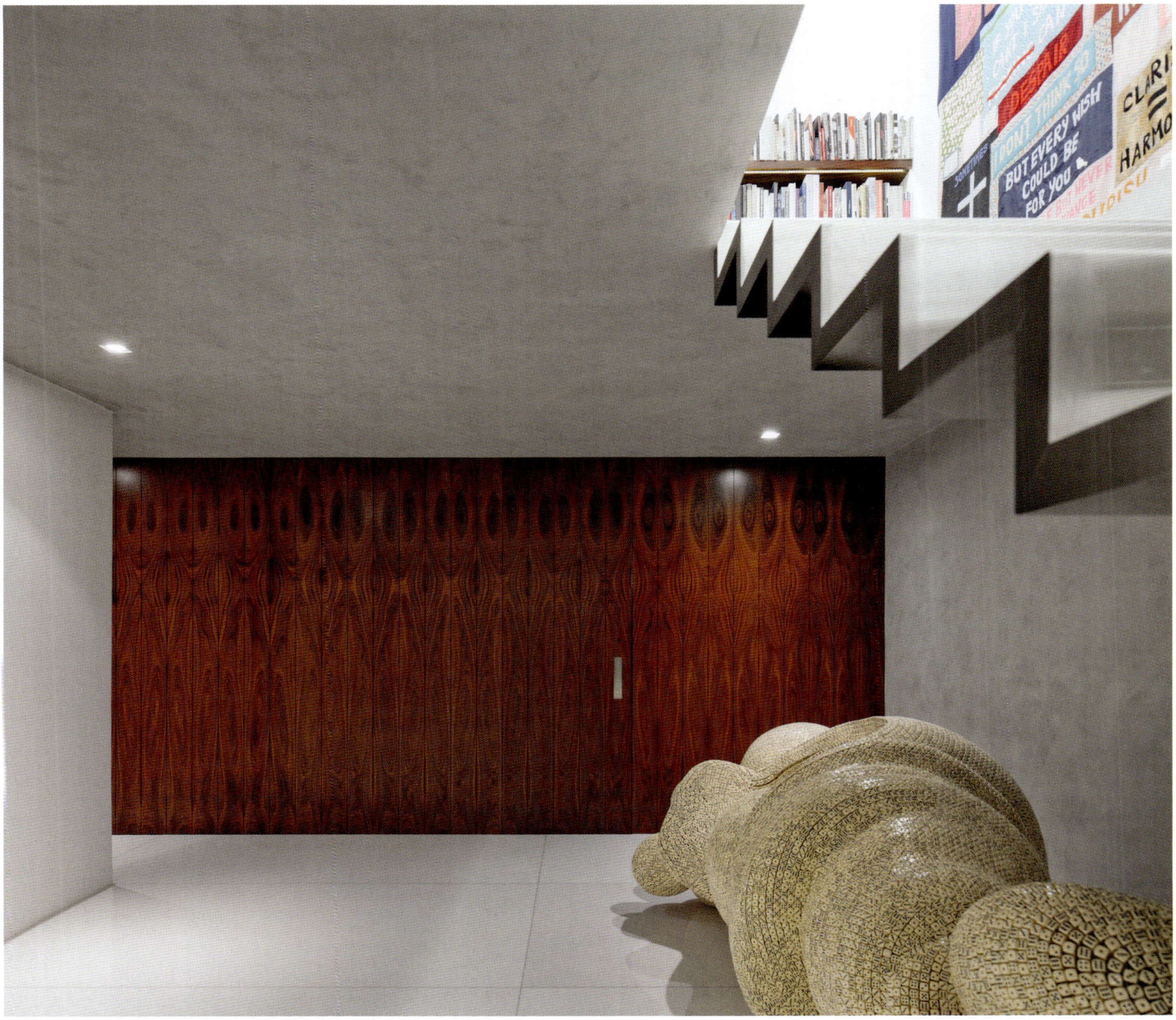
DESPAIR
I DON'T THINK SO
BUT EVERY WISH
COULD BE
FOR YOU

AUFBAU
RECONSTRUCTION
150 Meilen
Neue Pläne für
Freihäfen in Libyen
Neues jüdisches Leben in Italien

# GENESES HOUSE

Twentieth-century Brazilian architecture was all about daring geometry and fearless structures. This house accommodates a program of a 2,700 m² (29,060 ft.²) home for a family with an active social life. It is on a steep São Paulo lot and is organized on three levels.

From the street entrance, a wide ascending path leads around the eastern face amid a lush tropical garden. Passing under the cantilevered block of the top level, the path skirts along the retaining slope before climbing to the flat garden lawn facing the home's social area.

The top level is dedicated entirely to entertainment. A spacious room spans the full extension of the level and includes various living areas defined by the arrangement of furnishings. Wooden strips on the ceiling and floor accentuate the length of the space, while three prominent vertical elements punctuate the room: a suspended fireplace and two round pillars clad in stainless steel. Glass doors on either side open completely onto two verandas overlooking the garden. Adjacent to the main staircase, a red box volume houses a Japanese-style dining room, projecting outward toward the garden and standing out from the main façade.

All private quarters are one floor below. Here, circulation follows a long internal hallway cantilevered over the front garden, providing access to all bedrooms. The lowest floor contains the garage, the caretaker's quarters, and all supporting areas.

Geneses House is Brazilian architectural daring in service of thriving familial life.

**Location:**
São Paulo, Brazil
**Year:**
2011
**Photography:**
Fernando Guerra

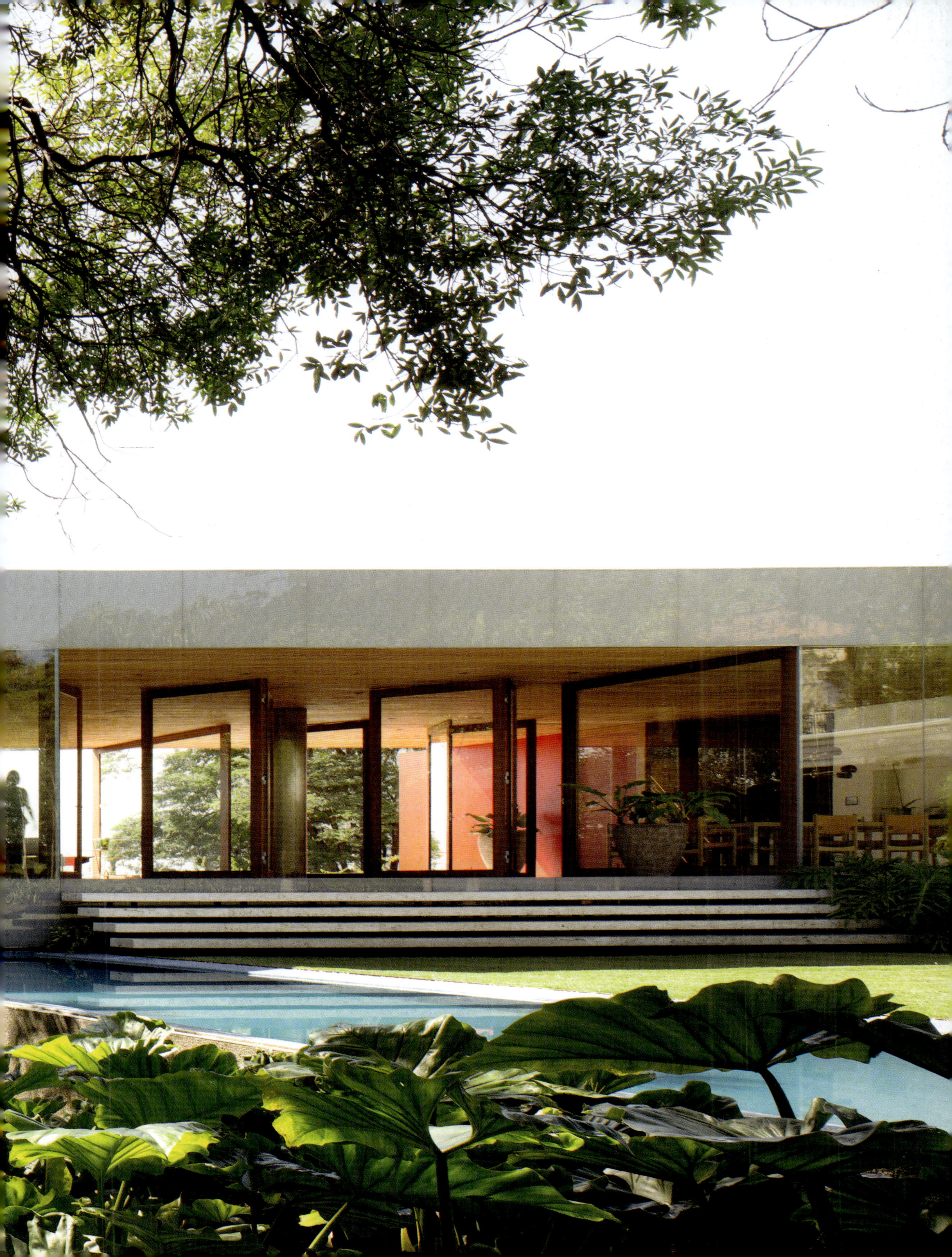

# PB HOUSE

As the largest city by population in the Western Hemisphere, São Paulo has its detractors—many calling it a "concrete jungle." However, Jardim Paulistano is a neighborhood within the city known for its parks and green spaces. For many Paulistanos, it is an urban refuge.

PB House is located in the residential district of Jardim Paulistano, occupying a corner plot. By aligning the construction parallel to the longer side of the plot, adjacent to the street, the scheme creates a linear garden at the rear, offering charming views for both private and entertaining areas. Overall, there is a feeling of the middle of the 20th century—Brazil's heyday.

On the ground floor, there is a sophisticated interplay of space and materials. Rooms are defined by varying levels and walls adorned with sleek black finishes. These walls, extending outward, are strategically positioned to draw attention to the outdoor surroundings. Minimalist aluminum frames, some fixed and others sliding, enhance the fluidity of space within the house. Moving to the upper floor reveals an all-white rectangular volume enveloped by mashrabiya screens.

Service areas are located underground, encompassing parking, a machinery room, servants' quarters, and a laundry room. The laundry room is arranged to open onto an inner courtyard, optimizing its functionality.

**Location:**
São Paulo, Brazil
**Year:**
2015
**Photography:**
Fernando Guerra

# ITALIA HOUSE

The placement of the house was driven by a desire that all rooms open onto a garden. As such, the access ramp to the underground parking, as well as the vertical circulation, were placed in the center of the lot. This allowed the social uses of the ground floor to develop around that core, always integrated with the external vegetation through glass frames.

Unexpected touches abound—like wood ceilings. An irregular design forms internal rooms and spacious external verandas. The exception is a single opaque volume: the powder room. It also stands out for its curved shape, softly delineating the entrance hall while affording privacy.

Private quarters are arranged between end walls and roof slabs of varying heights and sizes, always set back from the perimeter of the base, creating a wraparound ring of vegetation that brings the garden closer, even on the upper floor.

The pool is at the back of the densely planted lot. The gym was placed below the pool to avoid the presence of another volume on the ground level. There is natural lighting and ventilation throughout, facilitated by a landscaped patio next to the boundary wall. Access to the pool and gym is via a tunnel connected to the underground parking. A stone staircase blends into the garden and reveals the pool among the vegetation as you descend.

**Location:**
São Paulo, Brazil
**Year:**
2023
**Photography:**
Fran Parente

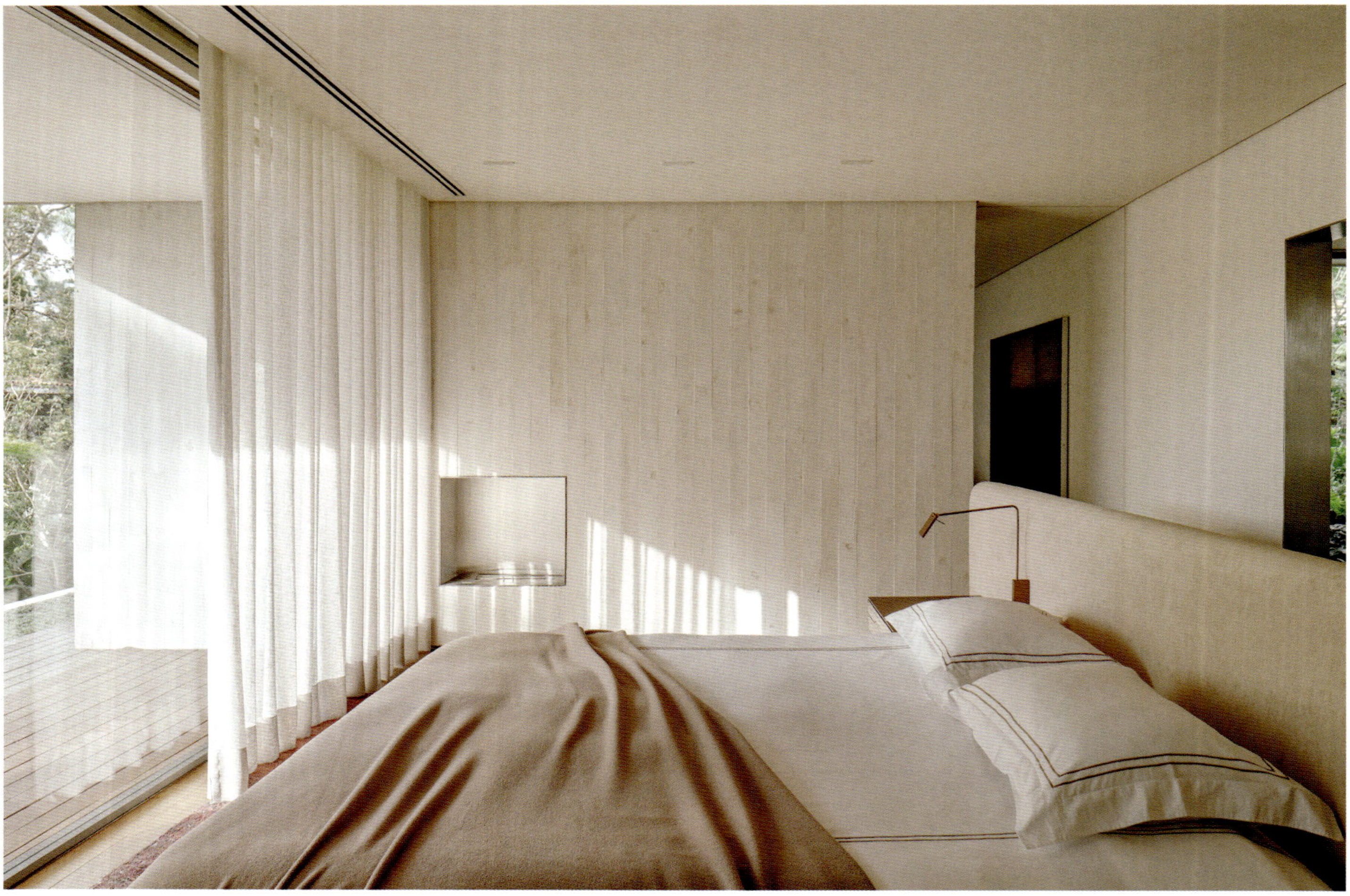

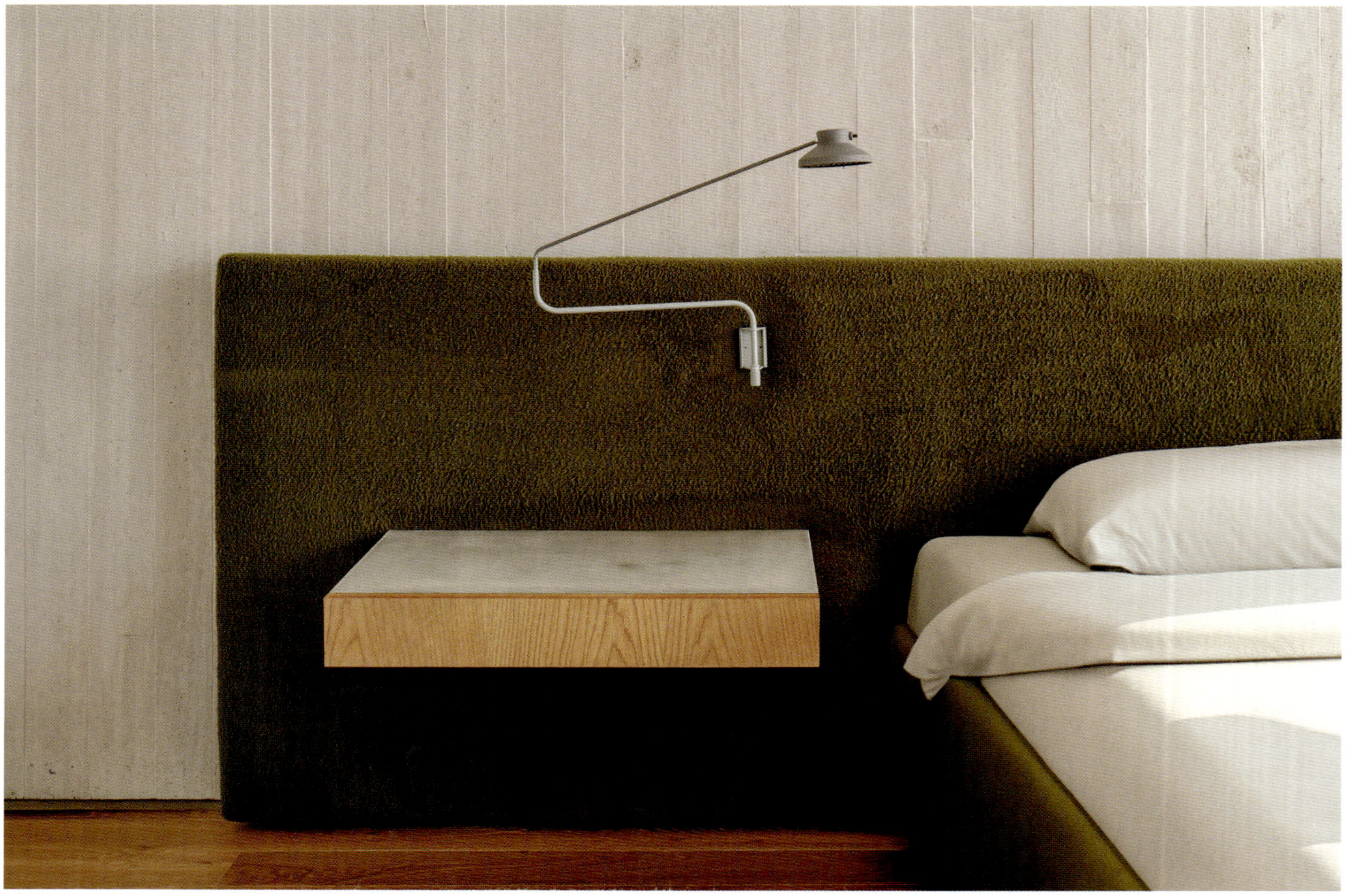

# WATER MILL HOUSE

Water Mill is an exclusive residential enclave within Southampton, on the eastern end of Long Island, New York. As one approaches Water Mill House from the street, a treelined driveway envelops the highest section of the land, guiding visitors to the house, which gradually comes into view amid two expansive strips of woods. At first glance, the house presents itself as an elongated glass prism crowned by an asymmetrical dual-pitched roof.

A modular structure, the house has a well-organized distribution of spaces. The kitchen occupies one module at the pavilion's end, while the adjacent module houses the entrance hall, powder room, and hallway. At the opposite end, three additional modules accommodate a mezzanine level and the dining and living rooms.

The lower floor is a striking contrast to the upper volume. It comprises six en suite bedrooms, a TV room, a multipurpose room, garage, technical areas, a spa, and an indoor pool. This solid, semi-buried base is entirely clad in rustic stone. Openings in the stone provide rhythm to the façade and establish a visual connection between the private areas and the garden and outdoor pool.

Occupants access the garden via an external staircase or directly from the bedrooms, where large glass doors open onto it. A spacious patio, situated at the center of the lower volume, serves to visually connect the circulation areas and the indoor pool.

In a community of wealth and privilege for New York's *beau monde*, Water Mill House stands out while fitting in.

**Location:**
Southampton, United States
**Year:**
2019
**Photography:**
Fernando Guerra

# 111 HOUSE

Located in São Paulo, 111 House is a haven for family life and entertaining friends. Commissioned by a couple with an extensive contemporary art collection, the house was conceived as both a backdrop for this collection and a place to raise their two thriving children.

To occupy a smaller portion of the lot and thus accommodate lush Brazilian foliage, the house unfolds over four floors. Transitioning from the street, a pergola-covered antechamber leads into a garden. The house then extends along the left side of the lot, almost to the rear boundary, where a gap allows light and natural ventilation into a lower-level patio. To the right, a lush garden spans the entire depth of the lot. The living room and informal dining rooms, as well as the upper-floor bedrooms, open to this green space.

The bedrooms and living rooms, facing northwest, are shielded from the afternoon sun by wide eaves and the walls separating the rooms, which also serve as sun breakers. These walls project outward to varying degrees perpendicularly to the façade, creating either fluid or integrated spaces on the ground floor, or more compartmentalized areas on the upper floor, according to their uses.

On the rooftop, a leisure area featuring a TV room and a solarium with a swimming pool, provides sweeping views of the surroundings.

The materials and gentle color palette throughout the house prioritize the residents' visual and tactile comfort. Extensive planters along the exterior openings on all floors create a dense ring of vegetation around the perimeter, ensuring the necessary protection and privacy. In sum, it is a green family refuge among the teeming streets of São Paulo.

**Location:**
São Paulo, Brazil
**Year:**
2022
**Photography:**
Fernando Guerra

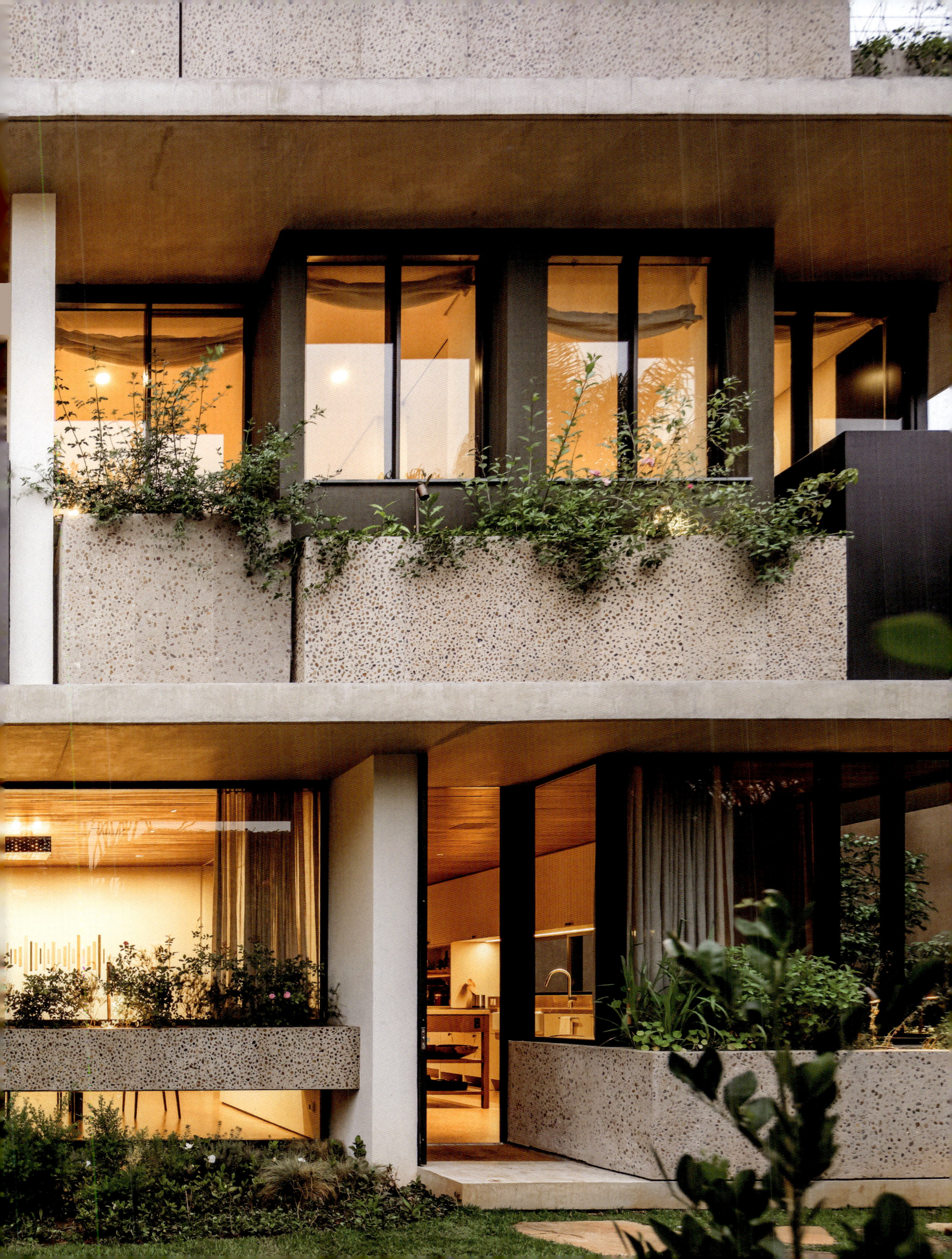

# SHERRY N APARTMENT

Located in the heart of Manhattan, at the southeast corner of Central Park, The Sherry-Netherland is both a hotel and cooperative apartment building and has been a luxury venue in the city for close to a century. The Sherry-Netherland has a signature copper roof and tall, slender massing. It is part of the Landmark Preservation Commission's Upper East Side Historic District.

The unit's modern design contrasts with the historic building. The clients combined multiple units to create a spacious single abode of nearly 500 m$^2$ (5,380 ft.$^2$). The apartment boasts views of Fifth Avenue, Central Park, 59th Street, and the adjacent Plaza Hotel.

Designers faced challenges designing in the landmarked structure—there were large shafts, pillars, and other structural elements that emerged after the old walls were demolished, dictating the configuration of the new floor plan. In the final layout, these elements were integrated into the cabinetry or clad in unconventional materials to blend with the new spaces, and large wall areas were cleared to display artwork.

From the foyer, a curved, polished, stainless-steel panel extends to the living room, creating a focal point and enhancing the sense of spaciousness. In addition to this mirrored panel, the walls in the main social areas are clad in walnut panels framing the windows and natural linen wallpaper. Other elements, such as a pillar covered in velvet and brass shelving units, complement the composition. The floors in the social areas and the kitchen are covered in Italian sandstone, while carpet was chosen for the floors in the private quarters, with more neutral shades on the walls. Bathrooms are clad in Prima marble, and the powder room features mirrored and natural walnut panels.

The furniture was selected to evoke environments from the 1960s and 1970s, as per the clients' request. Primarily using pieces by French designers, the designers introduced jolts of color. Some items, such as the dining room chandelier and sofas, were custom-made for the apartment. The finished space boasts a late 20th-century vibe in a building from New York's Gilded Age.

**Location:**
New York, United States
**Year:**
2020
**Photography:**
Fernando Guerra

# AB APARTMENT

A lively mid-century feel infuses this apartment in São Paulo. It has two floors: one houses bedrooms, a study, and the family room; the other contains the kitchen, laundry, dining room, leisure terrace, living room, space to display the family art collection, a screening room, and service areas.

Located on the 13th and 14th floors and affording privileged views of the city of São Paulo, both floors have an extensive terrace on the back façade of the building. This creates coziness within the vastness of the apartment, preserving the views but with terraces full of vegetation that visually extend into the home, where the city view is seen through the landscaping, creating a screen between the outside and the interior. On the upper floor, the social area, everything was done in Italian limestone, with various marbles in the bathrooms.

An entire module clad in suede delineates the living room, the screening room, and the family breakfast nook. The library, where wood prevails, extends along the side windows and embraces the view and the light. Additionally, the wood on the walls that delineate the center of the apartment has different finishes and shades. On the lower level, the private floor, reclaimed old wood was used on the floor.

The bathrooms were clad in different stones from Italy and Turkey. Two staircases were designed to connect the private and the social floors, one made of metal, the other of stone and wood. The interior and furniture design developed over two years, during several trips to the United States and Europe in search of modernist antiques, as well as anonymous pieces that would harmonize with the client's existing collection. A desk by Jean Gillon and an armchair by Zanine are among the pieces acquired. Other pieces, such as the dining room table and sideboard, were designed by Isay Weinfeld and his team, complementing the chairs by Axel Einar Hjorth and lamps by Alvar Aalto.

**Location:**
São Paulo, Brazil
**Year:**
2018
**Photography:**
Fernando Guerra

# DOS PATIOS HOUSE

Dos Pátios House was designed for a couple with two children in a leafy residential neighborhood in São Paulo. The plot is a long and narrow strip of land. Given this, and for better solar orientation, the house was placed along the right border, leaving the front and back areas for gardens. The main access to the house is on the left, under a wooden pergola amid lush greenery.

In addition to the family quarters, an annex accommodates a guest room and a gym connected to the recreation area. The house has three levels. The underground contains the garage, workshop, technical areas (water tank, pool pumps, water heater, generator), as well as the servants' quarters and laundry room, both opening onto a garden. The ground floor is reserved for all social areas, while the bedrooms and a private living room for the family are upstairs.

The house was built using a mixed structural system (reinforced concrete for the underground and ground levels, steel for the upper level). This assemblage provides the necessary support for the cantilever over the swimming pool terrace.

Solar heating panels were installed on the rooftop, along with skylights to provide natural lighting to the upper-level bathrooms and walk-in closet. Various patios and terraces on all levels allow for ample natural lighting and ventilation in every room.

**Location:**
São Paulo, Brazil
**Year:**
2013
**Photography:**
Leonardo Finotti

FIVE

# HIGH-RISE BUILDINGS

# GIRASSOL 555 BUILDING

Girassol 555 Building is a mixed-use complex that combines commercial spaces, a café, and a theater in a development located in the heart of Vila Madalena in western São Paulo.

The plot has a steep topography and irregular shape; it resulted from the merging of several smaller lots. This informed the project concept: three independent volumes, each situated on a different section of the land, with spaces for gardens and communal areas in between. This choice ensured abundant natural light for all units and created interesting visual connections among the towers and their surroundings. Above all, it prevented the construction of an overly bulky volume that would disrupt the neighborhood scale.

Access to the complex is through the blue tower on Rua Girassol. The ground floor, raised on stilts, doubles as a spacious welcoming plaza, connecting the street to the offices. Open to both passersby and building occupants, it features a café and a large seating area, also serving as access and foyer to the theater located one level below. The access control to the offices—including reception and turnstiles—is centralized under the same stilted plaza, slightly beyond the communal area.

The three towers, each with different proportions, house a total of 64 units ranging from 111 to 850 m$^2$ (1,195 to 9,150 ft.$^2$), which can be combined to create larger units. On the exterior, foliage spills from the rooftops and balconies.

The structural framework, comprising pigmented concrete in blue, green, or pink, is the strongest identity element of the complex. This identity is furthered by a modulation that lends rhythm to the façades and is consistent across all three towers.

**Location:**
São Paulo, Brazil
**Year:**
2019
**Photography:**
Leonardo Finotti

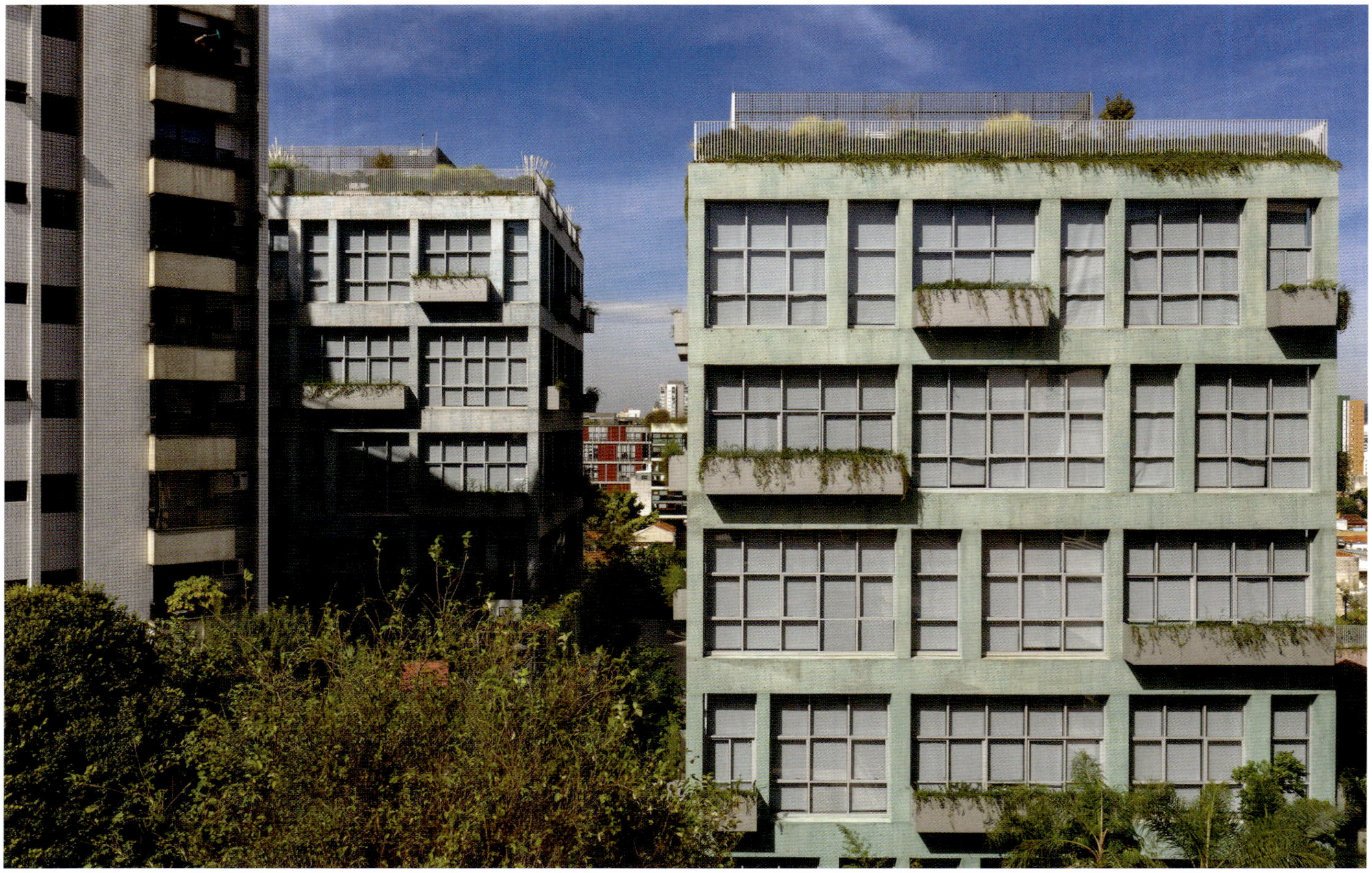

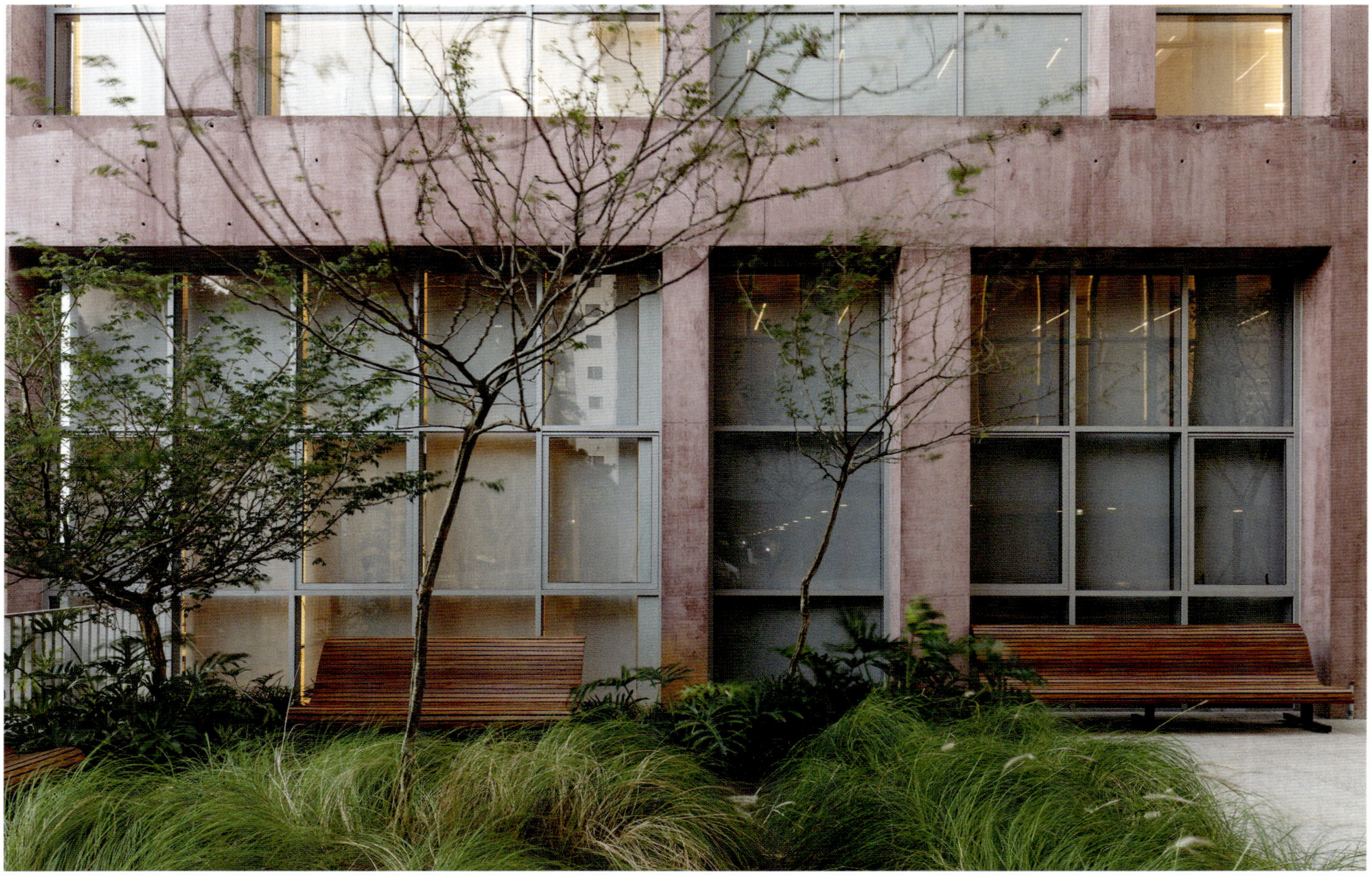

# SANTOS AUGUSTA BUILDING

The Santos Augusta Building, at the corner of Rua Augusta and Alameda Santos in São Paulo, faces Conjunto Nacional, in the high-rise area along Avenida Paulista. From its vantage point, the building enjoys a privileged view overlooking the Pinheiros River valley and the city's lush Jardins neighborhood.

The most striking aspect of the building is its cantilevered massing. Comprising four stacked volumes of varying sizes and proportions, the tower hovers above a large ground-level plaza that serves as an extension of the sidewalk. This plaza, bordered by gardens and outdoor seating areas, seamlessly integrates with the lobby and café space through the opening of expansive sliding doors. The building reception and theater box office are in the lobby, providing independent access to both the offices and the theater.

The first volume, spanning the 1st to the 3rd floors, houses the theater and its supporting facilities, including dressing rooms, storage areas, a foyer, and restrooms. The second and third volumes, from the 5th to the 9th and 11th to the 17th floors, respectively, are reserved for office suites, and each floor can be subdivided into two units, each with an adjoining covered terrace.

At the tower's pinnacle, the fourth volume (19th and 20th floors) accommodates the mezzanine of the rooftop office suite and a technical floor.

Between each volume, there is a transitional floor where the building façade is set back on all four sides, creating a wraparound terrace and emphasizing the distinctiveness of each volume. These transitional floors house a restaurant on the 4th floor, a 450 m$^2$ (4,844 ft.$^2$) office suite on the 10th, and the lower level of the duplex suite on the 18th.

While all four volumes are clad in the same material—brownstone, a type of sandstone—the arrangement and finish of the stones vary. Five underground parking levels complete the development, providing 389 spaces allocated to both the offices and the theater.

**Location:**
São Paulo, Brazil
**Year:**
2018
**Photography:**
Fernando Guerra

# 360º BUILDING

360º Building is located in São Paulo, the most populous city in the Western Hemisphere. Perched atop a ridge between the Alto de Pinheiros and Alto da Lapa districts, 360º Building offers residents breathtaking views of the surrounding area and cityscape.

In this urban landscape, it's common for residents to endure cramped living spaces and lengthy commutes. Leisure opportunities are limited, and outdoor activities are scarce. Recognizing the challenges of Brazilian urban living, designers conceived 360º Building as an alternative to the conventional vertical multifamily housing model. Unlike the typical stacked apartment units, it offers a different approach.

How so? With 62 elevated homes featuring real yards—not mere balconies—the building provides spacious, airy living spaces designed to enhance residents' quality of life. These homes range from 130 or 170 m² to 250 or 415 m² (1,400 or 1,830 ft.² to 2,690 or 4,470 ft.²), combined in sets of two, three, or four units per floor, in six different arrangements. They are available in multiple configurations, catering to different needs and preferences.

Residents are first greeted by a suspended walkway leading to the building's lobby, encircled by a reflecting pool. The ground level has entertainment areas, a gym, a lounge, a function room, and laundry facilities. The lowest level houses employee quarters, storage, engine rooms, a sauna, and an outdoor swimming pool. The building's design takes advantage of the steep slope of the land, allowing lower levels to be subterranean—making them cool in summer and warm in winter.

360º Building fully integrates with its surroundings, with no distinction between main and secondary façades. It embodies a holistic approach to urban living that prioritizes spaciousness, functionality, and comfort.

**Location:**
São Paulo, Brazil
**Year:**
2013
**Photography:**
Fernando Guerra

# OITO BUILDING

Oito Building stands distinctively on a sloping plot in Vila Madalena, a district of São Paulo. It commands views of two streets with a 15-meter (49-foot) elevation difference between both ends. A quaint square lies opposite the building, while a row of low-rise houses meanders down the sloping contour toward the Pinheiros River.

Architects embraced the plot's personality while adhering to the city's building regulations. The ground level of the building—its main access—is situated at the higher end, with eight levels rising above and another five levels below ground. This strategic positioning ensures that even the semi-buried levels below the ground floor enjoy vistas from three open façades.

Approaching from the street, a striking marquee guides visitors to the main lobby, located 20 meters (65 feet) above the lower end of the land, offering panoramic views of the surroundings. The building's architectural identity is a metal frame constructed from a modulated orthogonal mesh, with a central axis housing the vertical circulation elements, thus maximizing the use of space.

Each layout has been thought out well, with living and dining areas oriented westward, overlooking the square, while bedrooms face eastward toward a quieter street. In the basement duplex, both social areas and bedrooms have views of the square. A wraparound terrace serves all levels and provides each room with a small outdoor extension.

Oito Building, quiet and self-effacing, integrates with its surroundings, offering residents not only a home but a unique connection to the neighborhood of Vila Madalena.

**Location:**
São Paulo, Brazil
**Year:**
2014
**Photography:**
Fernando Guerra

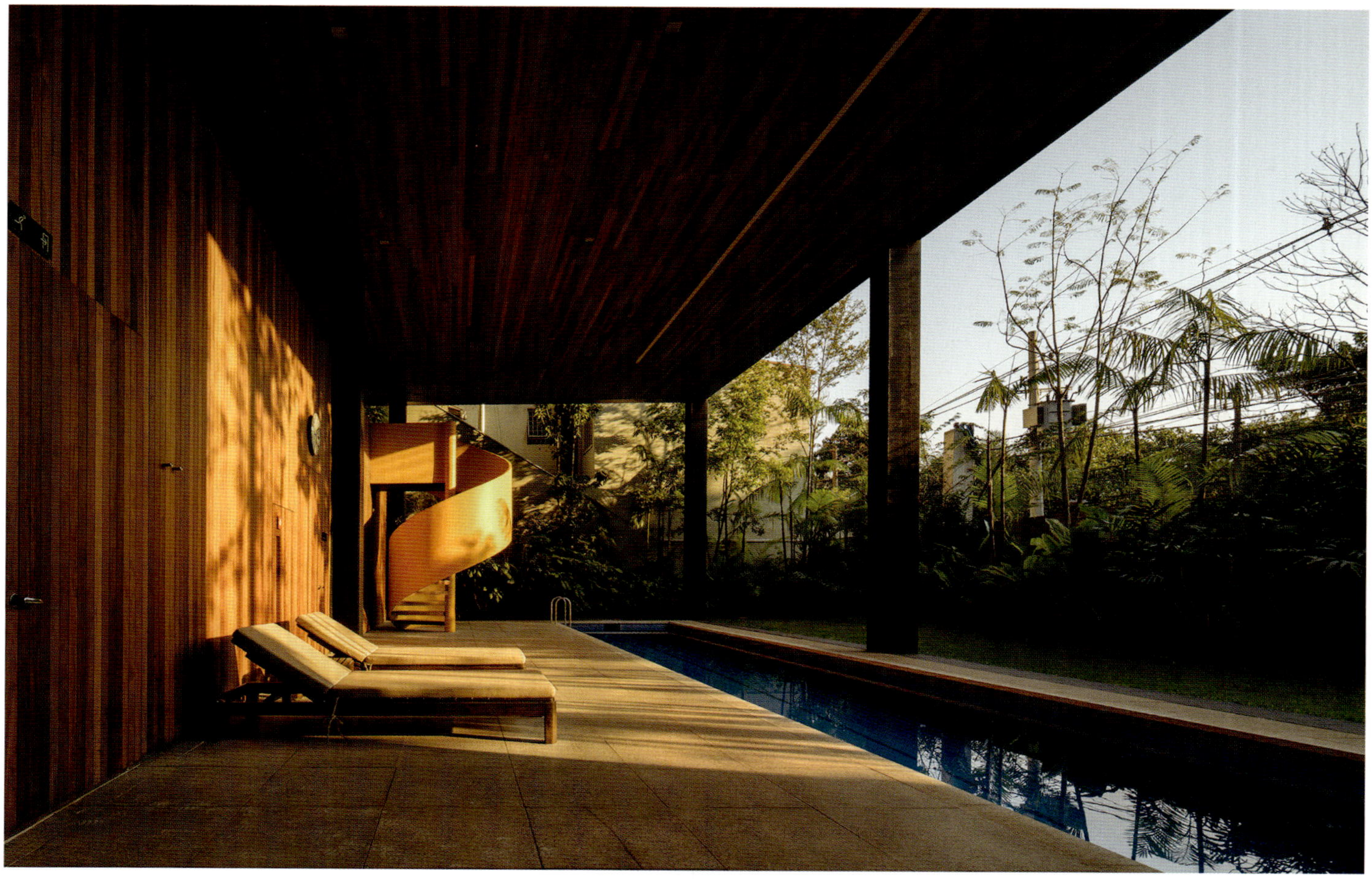

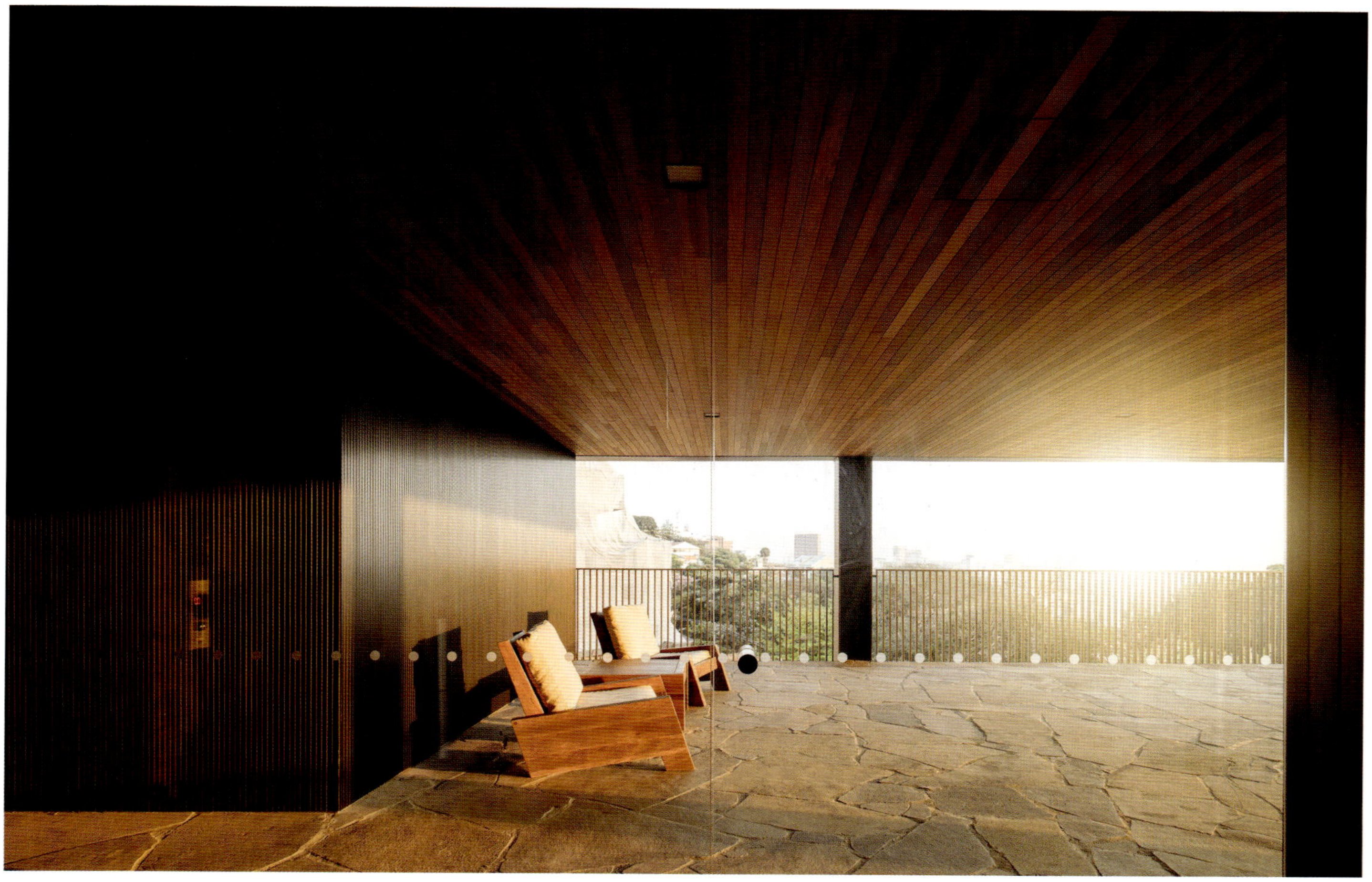

# AZUL BUILDING

Another Vila Madalena São Paulo residential high-rise, Azul Building is nestled on a lot between Rua Simpatia and Rua Medeiros de Albuquerque. The unique shape and topography of the lot played a pivotal role in determining the building's layout and mixed-use program.

From Rua Simpatia, a lengthy walkway guides residents and visitors to the residential block, thoughtfully aligned along its central axis. The tower itself is a study in balance and ingenuity, composed of two volumes with trapezoidal plans, elegantly overlapped in a symmetrical, inverted manner. Each volume, distinguished by its distinct color palette, accommodates one apartment per floor, with exceptions made for the duplex and penthouse units, which span two floors each.

Every apartment within Azul Building has a generously sized balcony that extends toward the streets, flooding the interiors with natural light and fresh air.

A third, lower volume attached to the complex houses the pool, parking, and commercial spaces, seamlessly integrated with the urban fabric. The design ethos of Azul Building is one of simplicity and functionality, with a careful balance struck among programmatic requirements, zoning regulations, and technical considerations.

**Location:**
São Paulo, Brazil
**Year:**
2016
**Photography:**
Fernando Guerra
Nelson Kon

# OKA BUILDING

The Oka Building is an innovative residential high-rise in the Vila Madalena district of São Paulo. At first glance, it appears to be a massing of concrete "boxes" bedecked with foliage.

To foster a harmonious relationship with its surroundings, the Oka Building cascades its levels in harmony with the contours of the land. Landscape integrates with building, creating a symbiotic relationship between nature and architecture. From a shared structural framework, each floor is arranged in a staggered manner, offering varied floor plans and layouts that cater to different needs.

The main entrance is positioned at the higher end of the lot on tranquil Rua Senador Cesar Lacerda Vergueiro. Above this level, five floors house spacious apartments, each approximately 420 m² (4,520 ft.²). At the pinnacle of the building there is a triplex penthouse with a sprawling 800 m² (8,610 ft.²) of living space.

Two duplex units face the lower street and offer captivating views over the treetops. Two amenity levels feature a gym, a sports court, a sauna, a swimming pool, and locker rooms. Finally, at street level on Rua Girassol, where traffic and activity are more pronounced, a 150 m² (1,615 ft.²) retail space with private parking completes the assemblage, adding a touch of convenience and functionality to this vibrant urban setting.

**Location:**
São Paulo, Brazil
**Year:**
2017
**Photography:**
Fernando Guerra
Leonardo Finotti

# MARQUÊS DE ITU BUILDING | HOUSING

The Marquês de Itu Building, located in São Paulo, is an apartment building developed under Minha Casa Minha Vida (MCMV), a public housing funding program. A key aspect of the economic feasibility strategy within MCMV's framework is the simultaneous development of projects to optimize resources and allow for the bulk purchase of materials at lower prices, resulting in constructive standardization wherever possible.

In this context, the construction system (structural masonry) and elements (from window frames to finishes) are predetermined for the project, regardless of the site and specific program. The choice of land—always centrally located, with easy access to public transportation—is another factor that reduces overall project costs by eliminating the need for parking levels and expensive basements.

The 690 m$^2$ (7,430 ft.$^2$) lot, located next to the Minhocão overpass at the corner of Rua Marquês de Itu and Avenida Amaral Gurgel, was studied under MCMV's guidelines, the Land Usage and Occupation Legislation, and the developer's requirements. The building was aligned with the sidewalk and separated from neighboring buildings to allow for sunlight and ventilation, with commercial venues opening directly onto the sidewalk, and a generous garden at the rear, sheltered from avenue traffic.

The ground floor, where a concrete structure molded on-site allows for larger spans, houses the entrance lobby, technical areas, and three apartment units—in addition to two shops. From the first floor upward, 15 typical floors laid out around the structural masonry accommodate eight apartment units each, including studios and one- and two-bedroom units, ranging from 24 to 35 m$^2$ (258 to 376 ft.$^2$).

The apartment units on the typical floors are positioned to maximize sunlight and views, facing the overpass—or Parque Minhocão. The open-air circulation corridors at the rear façade allow for cross-ventilation in the units and free the main façade from the mandatory permanent gas ventilation louvers.

The common areas—a function room, laundry room, workroom, gardens, and vegetable garden—are on the rooftop, so that all residents can enjoy the expansive city views from the top floor, slightly removed from the hustle and bustle of the street and overpass.

**Location:**
São Paulo, Brazil
**Year:**
2021
**Photography:**
Fernando Guerra

# VARANDA BUILDING

The Varanda Building is an apartment building located in Porto Alegre in southern Brazil. The local Land Use and Occupation Legislation, which allows construction without setbacks at street level, was crucial in shaping the architectural concept—a tower rising on stilts from a base volume that occupies the entire perimeter of the lot.

Forming this base volume, the street level is entirely covered by a slab dotted with openings that bring natural light to the various gardens, patios, and leisure spaces below. A wooden deck weaves through regularly spaced pillars over a reflecting pool amid a lush garden, whose contours widen or narrow according to the use—a lounge by the pool, a playground, and a barbecue area. Small volumes contain restrooms and vertical circulation shafts, leaving the rest of the space open, only partially sheltered by the projection of the tower.

A delicate marquee jutting from this volume onto the sidewalk marks the entrance to the building. It leads inside to the entry lobby, where a sitting set by Brazilian furniture designers the Campana Brothers takes up the room. The building boasts extensive leisure facilities, comfortably accommodated on the ground and stilted levels, leaving the tower itself for the residential units.

The tower houses 26 apartment units over 14 floors, ranging from 300 to 615 m² (3,230 to 6,620 ft.²). The typical floor has two three-bedroom units, from the 1st to the 12th floor. The top two floors accommodate three- and four-bedroom apartments, each occupying an entire floor with generous layouts and various social spaces, including a private pool on the 14th-floor unit.

All apartments open to generous balconies facing the northwest, offering sunset views of the city skyline.

**Location:**
Porto Alegre, Brazil
**Year:**
2023
**Photography:**
Fernando Guerra

# LA PETITE AFRIQUE BUILDING

In the heart of Monaco's Monte Carlo district, La Petite Afrique is a residential building that brings a Brazilian sensibility to the Mediterranean Côte d'Azur. Located adjacent to the gardens of Casino de Monte Carlo and just a block away from the landmark Hotel de Paris and Salle Garnier, the building is in a privileged location. The surrounding streets, local topography, mixed-use program and upscale character of the building informed early design decisions.

From the outset, the project prioritized views of the adjacent gardens and the Mediterranean Sea. Each floor is enveloped by balcony gardens, seamlessly merging the outdoor scenery with the indoor living spaces. Crafted from sand-colored limestone solids, the balconies enhance the aesthetic appeal of the building and integrate it harmoniously with Monte Carlo's urban context.

The private entrance to the apartments is on Avenue de la Madone, a calm curvilinear road that slopes uphill by the gardens of the casino. La Petite Afrique's main lobby offers views of the neighboring gardens. The ground level on Boulevard des Moulins provides access to cafés and retail spaces and serves as the entrance to the commercial space. This versatile square footage can accommodate multiple users or a single large company. On the first basement level, residents have a private spa, where natural light filters in through roof lights.

The meticulously designed apartments occupy entire floors, except for the second floor, whose unit shares space with the commercial area. Atop the building, an expansive penthouse duplex occupies the two top floors and includes a roof terrace with a large pool, offering views of the surrounding urban landscape and the sea beyond.

**Location:**
Monte Carlo, Monaco
**Year:**
2017
**Photography:**
Fernando Guerra

# JARDIM BUILDING

Nestled in the heart of New York's Chelsea neighborhood, just steps from the High Line, Jardim occupies a prime location spanning 27th and 28th Streets.

The building's 36 apartments are located in two towers, each with its own character. One tower is along 27th Street and the other along 28th Street, both sharing a base. A spacious tunnel traverses this base, seamlessly connecting the two streets and providing access to the lobby, which overlooks a garden.

A level above, a second garden oasis divides the two towers. The tower facing 28th Street spans the width of the plot, harmoniously integrating with neighboring buildings and continuing the plane of façades along the street. By contrast, the tower on 27th Street boasts a more compact, stand-alone design, offering glimpses of the rear tower and the adjacent elevated garden.

Despite their unique architectural profiles, the towers share an identity through the use of exposed brick and concrete. The building fits the urban context of Chelsea, known as a hip district of galleries, restaurants, and bars.

**Location:**
New York, United States
**Year:**
2020
**Photography:**
Fernando Guerra

SIX

# APPENDIX

# ISAY WEINFELD

São Paulo, Brazil (1952)

Isay Weinfeld is the Head Architect of a studio that takes his name and has been based in São Paulo, Brazil, since its founding in 1973.

After graduating from Universidade Presbiteriana Mackenzie in 1975, Weinfeld has run a multidisciplinary practice focused on projects across diverse areas—office, civic, commercial, residential, hospitality, etc.—always providing full architecture and interior design services.

Among countless projects developed over the years, some of the highlights are the hotels designed for Grupo Fasano in São Paulo, Punta del Este, and Porto Feliz, La Petite Afrique Building in Monaco, and the Jardim Building and Le Pavillon, the latter for Daniel Boulud in New York City, in addition to the feature film *Fogo e Paixao* and a line of office furniture designed for Geiger/Herman Miller.

Weinfeld has received many awards over a career spanning more than 50 years, such as the MIPIM AR Future Projects Awards organized by British magazine *Architectural Review* (for 360º Building in 2009, and for Oka Building in 2012).

His work has been featured in numerous publications in Brazil and abroad, including monographs written by journalists Daniel Piza (2006), Raul Barreneche (2008 and 2012), and Shonquis Moreno (2018).

Isay Weinfeld extends his gratitude to every individual who played a role in the development of the projects showcased in this book, with special recognition for Adriana Aun, Adriana Marcus, Adriana Zampieri, Alan Chu, Alexandre Nobre, Ana Luisa C. Pinheiro, Anthony Ling, Bruno Levy, Carolina Gimenez, Carolina Maluhy, Carolina Miranda, Cristiano Kato, Daniel Arce, Daniela Kurc, Daniela Hoffrichter, Danilo Hideki, Danilo Zamboni, Domingos Pascali, Eduardo Lisboa, Eduardo Chalabi, Elena Scarabotolo, Elisa Canjani, Eva Tsouni, Fabio Rudnik, Fausto Natsui, Felipe Hess, Felipe Zene, Fernando Mendonça, Flavia Oide, Gabriel Bicudo, Gabriel Fiuza, Gabriela Chow, Guilherme Leme, Gustavo Benthien, Ilza Fujimura, Isis Chaulon, João Matos, João Neri, Joara Pereira, Juliana Garcia, Juliana Scalizi, Katherina Ortner, Leandro Garcia, Lucas Jimeno Dualde, Luciana Siqueira, Lúcio Olivier, Manoel Maia, Marcela Aleotti, Marcelo Alvarenga, Marcelo Ribas, Mariana Vilela, Marília Franco, Marina Capocchi, Monica Cappa, Nara Diniz, Natalie Carvalho, Nilton Suenaga, Nina Ketelaars, Nuno Pinho, Pablo Alvarenga, Pablo Resende, Pedro Dias, Pedro Ricciardi, Políminia Garro, Priscila Araújo, Relbert Amorim, Sara Leitão, Sarkis Semerdjian, Sebastian Murr, Shinobu Kamimura, Sophia Lin, Thiago Moretti, Tiago Lambuça, Tiago Mestre, Tiago Rodrigues, and Wellington Diogo. In addition, the architect offers heartfelt thanks to the esteemed clients whose trust made these projects possible. Finally, deep appreciation is expressed to Gregorio Avila, Mariana Nakiri, and the teams at Oscar Riera Ojeda Publishers and Rizzoli for their contributions to the production of this publication.

**Book Credits**

Compilation by Mariana Nakiri
Art Direction by Oscar Riera Ojeda
Graphic Design by Juan Pablo Sarrabayrouse
Front and Back Cover Photography by Fernando Guerra

Printed in Hong Kong
2025 2026 2027 2028/ 10 9 8 7 6 5 4 3 2 1

Visit us online:
Instagram.com/RizzoliBooks
Facebook.com/RizzoliNewYork
X: @Rizzoli_Books
Youtube.com/user/RizzoliNY